I0816199

Published by Familius LLC, www.familius.com

PO Box 1130, Sanger, CA 93657

Familius books are available at special discounts for bulk purchases, whether for sales promotions or for family or corporate use. For more information, contact Familius Sales at orders@familius.com.

Photography sourced from Wikimedia Commons.

Leaf pattern sourced from Vecteezy.com

Library of Congress Control Number: 2025935382

Print ISBN 9798893960075

Ebook ISBN 9798893960785

Printed in China

Edited by Paige Adams, Gretchen Picklesimer Kinney, and Leah Welker

Cover design by Carlos Mireles-Guerrero and Brooke Jorden

Book design by Brooke Jorden

10 9 8 7 6 5 4 3 2 1

First Edition

FOUR WALKS IN CENTRAL PARK

A Poetic Guide to the Park

Aaron Poochigian

By Phil Whitehouse from London, United Kingdom –
The Arcade at Bethesda Terrace, Central Park

In Memory of Frederick Olmsted, Architect of Central Park

Some artists work in spiraling claymation;
others in sultry bronze or trusty oils.
You, though, like on the third day of Creation,
made a world from waters, rocks and soils.

PROLOGUE:
The Invitation

We struggle, but there's always Central Park
offering water that upholds and bark
to lean on. People need its long, lake-flecked
recovery, its routes and shoots and birds.

Writers, you know, they leave their worlds of words,
but Frederick Olmsted, landscape architect,
and his ingenious right hand Calvert Vaux
left us a good-sized earth as their bequest.
The public rectangle runs fifty blocks
from north to south, a half mile east to west.

I know that headshake, like you're asking, "Why?
Why sacrifice Manhattan real estate?"

America deserved its own Versailles,
one not grown only for a potentate.
We needed both groomed lanes where a tycoon
with coattails could parade his horse and buggy
and lawns where clerks and maids could meet and talk
outside their tenements and off the clock.
We needed more than bathhouse or saloon.

So blueprints, pumps and shovels turned dank, muggy
acreage to a New World paradise
that grants asylum where the concrete ends,
and yet you've never been there.
                                        We've been friends
since make-believe back home in yards of yore.
I know you too well. Time for some advice:

because you haven't left your office much
for years and don't try new things anymore,
play hooky—yes, fake sick—and we'll explore
that curious retreat.
                              The sheep and gneiss
and willow trees will get us back in touch
with texture. Holidays outside the box
are what keep people from the loony bin.

I've got it all planned out. Four days, four walks
redressing stress, gloom, burnout and deflation.
Four days of trails and tales and recreation;
four days at large.
                              We'll quest beyond time clocks
and worldly wages for the Cheshire grin.

What do you say?
                              You'll do it?
                                              Yay.
                                                          You're in.

WALK ONE:
For the Overworked

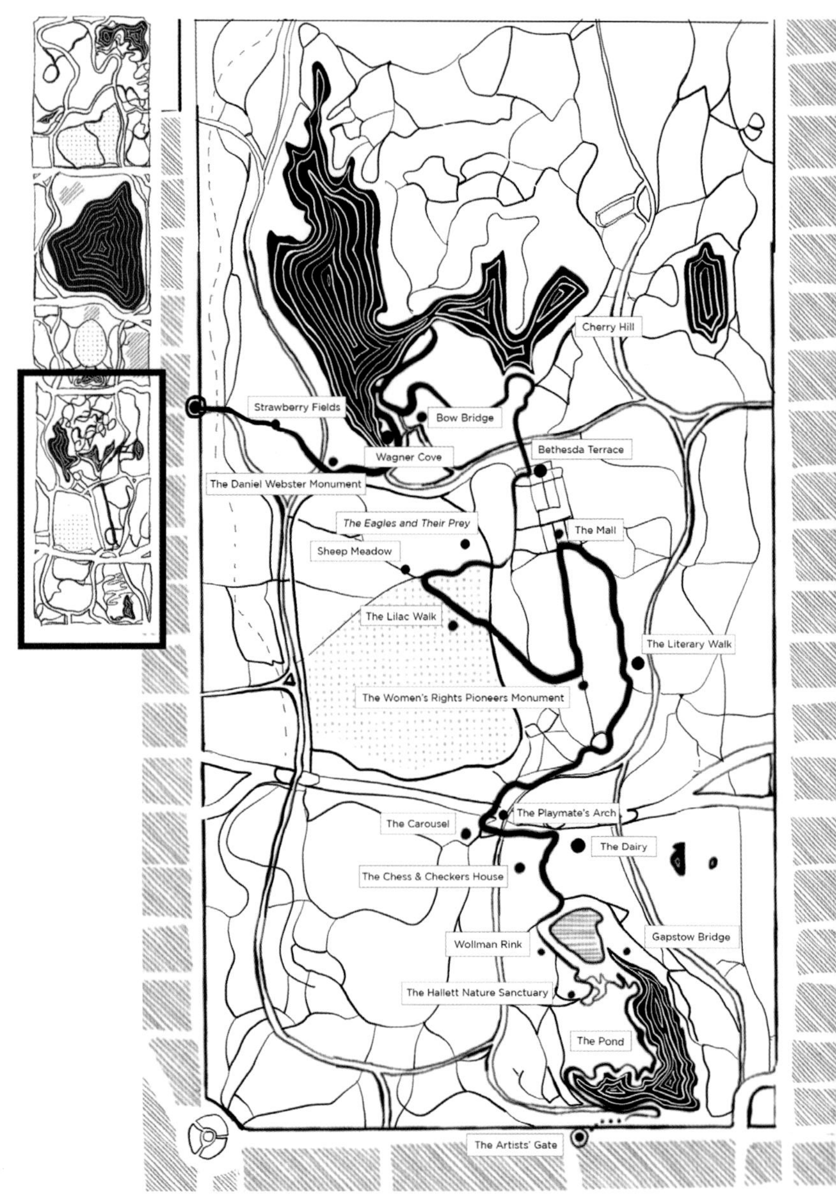

Start: 6th Ave and 59th St

The Artists' Gate

After a good run parting a ravine
of signs and high-rises, Sixth Avenue
terminates at the simple Artists' Gate.

To enter here, friend, we must travel through
the shadows of José de San Martín,
José Martí and Simón Bolívar,
bronze rebels riding mettlesome bronze horses.
They charged the guns of kings to liberate
the New World from the Old. How fierce they are,
how scornful of the world's restrictive forces.
The never-blinking trio of them sits
provocatively opposite the Ritz
to zone communal wealth off from its rival.
They guard land sanctified for the revival
of mind and body. Greet them as we pass.

Why not go barefoot and appraise the grass
now that the *joie de vivre* has begun?
Already there's a cushy rock formation
turning to soothing stone beneath the sun.
Just lean back and survey our vast vacation.

So many: stretching, straying, on a run.
They come from tension to the Center Drive—
everyone from the flushest to the poorest

toilers and fretters—then they come alive,
and you are one more here among them like
the hero of a fairy-tale beginning
a journey through the metamorphic forest.

It's not a race (you are already winning),
so how would you prefer to travel? Bike?
E-scooter? Moped? Rickshaw? Horse-drawn carriage?
All of them have their perks. I won't disparage
revving or coasting, cantering or spinning,
but recommend, most humbly, we should walk,
like, at an easy pace. You know, like, stroll.
That way we wide-eyed connoisseurs can talk
about the visions this ambitious outing
delivers without sputtering or shouting.

Alright, then: feet are how we're going to roll.

The Pond

Leaving the main path for an eastbound lane
that runs past boulders into damp terrain,
we stroll along the south shore of the Pond.
Suddenly in seclusion, we enjoy
the hushed proximity of rock and frond,
buoyant nitella and flamboyant koi.

I know you work long hours at a computer
and vow solemnly, every New Year's Day,
to get out there and do it, be a looter
at last of life's elusive spice and play.
There is the anarch urge to dive from dry land
into the green release of it, a fertile
profundity, and glide out to an island
where strutting egrets and an age-old turtle
are off the clock. You'd stay there all day long,
just being free, and then, in afterglow,
swim back ashore and, muddy in the rushes,
assist Louisiana waterthrushes
in the solemnity of sexy song . . .

since that won't happen, listen: take it slow.
Hear how the laughs of ducks and brass of geese
only contribute to the greater peace
by hushing deadline dread and sedentary
angst from the long days.
                                        First there are the trees—
a corrugated yew, a seamless beech,
ginormous oak and dwarfish serviceberry.
Then humans happen: somber retirees
start giggling at a pigtailed Pekinese,
and raucous moms distractedly beseech
kids not to shout and please behave their best.

"Hush, now, and take in Nature."
"See; don't tease."

Eased after passing ordinarily stressed
and festinate Manhattanites at ease,
we mount a flight of fieldstone steps and reach
a span, the first of many.

Gapstow Bridge

Vine-caressed,
romance-exuding Gapstow Bridge connects
the manmade wild exploding to the west
with the main path that runs around the Pond.
Its gentle vault jumps water that reflects
that vault in ripples. Visitors are fond
of snapping selfies here because they sense
this crannied crossing is of consequence.

"I just got photobombed by butterflies."

"The asters match the lilacs in your eyes."

Just standing on a vantage feels like glory;
high points abide as cardinal memories.

The Hallett Nature Sanctuary

This forest starting where the stone suspense
ends is the Hallett Nature Sanctuary,
a slow knoll most still call the "Promontory."
Luxuriant in leaves and lapidary
benches, it delivers instant ease
and just keeps deepening. Let's walk the path
north of the Pond and take a "forest-bath"
(that's *shinrin yoku* in the Japanese).

Now we are fully under. Stroll and listen
to hush and the hypnotic melodies
of gnatcatchers and nighthawks. Sit and watch
sunlight through living ceiling dim and glisten
tints of green. Bathe, bathe—that's what this swatch
of wilderness is for.
Mulberry, birch,
wisteria and ash, close-growing trees,
weave twilight even when the day is sunny.
When I walk here alone, I get that funny
frisson that sneaks up in an empty church.
You know, like something science just can't square
has breached the boundary and is in the air.
Notice how those we meet, like monks and nuns,
are whispering in awe, and we are, too.

We could just wander through this monastery
till Kingdom Come, but our itinerary
insists we get a move-on.

Wollman Rink

So we do:
back in the sun, we walk the path that runs
just west of the alfresco Wollman Rink.
Spring, summer, autumn—they're for roller skating.
No more reclusion, no more sacred stasis.
This oval parties down. Here's what I think:
you should come here some night for DiscOasis.
There will be people meeting, people dating,
and you among them, boogying in sync
to Rick James, Lipps Inc. and The Outhere Brothers.

And if you end up on your butt, who cares?
Just clamber over to the outside wall,
inch upward and rejoin the sway of others
circling, circling en masse, in pairs
and solo like they are the disco ball.
Those wild nights wheel as one.

The Chess & Checkers House

From there we weave
through sheen and shade down interlocking lanes
past Weymouth pines, mushrooms and London planes.
The rise starts slow but, when we leave the muddy
flats near the rink, an asphalt ramp up rock
inclines our steps toward steeps whose heights upheave
the striped and steepled octagon they call
the Chess & Checkers House. Here anybody
can check out any of the stuff in stock:
gameboards and timers, chessmen, pairs of dice.

Tell me: you ever played for stakes at all?
Till sunset here the gentlemanly vice
keeps pulses pounding, and of course the cops
don't care about guys playing for a buck
or fiver.
"Double jump!" a general yawps,
then levels, "Deadlock. All your men are stuck."

All round the house, beneath a timber trellis,
benches on either side of tabletops
(each one a battered chessboard) creak as zealous
beginners, hungry amateurs and pros
determine, wordlessly, who's got the chops.
Pawns foremost to the fight like beach marines,
devious bishops, bastions like backhoes,

swaggering knights and all-round lethal queens
leap, glide and plod about the staggered squares,
knocking off foes until resistance grows
ridiculous. *Checkmate!* A king despairs.

Still others like to link up dominoes.

We scuff back down, then swivel northeast on
a path that winds between greenwood and lawn.
An oak approaches, and a suave voice airs,
as if in greeting, a concatenary
concert of coos. It's rare: a white-winged dove.

The Dairy

Our next landmark receives us with unwary
earnestness, like it should be in Vermont
among robust Holsteins. The proud child of
Victorian Gothic and a barn, the Dairy
served in its first years as a public font
of milk for kids and grown-ups, for all comers,
back when the wholesome stuff was hard to find.
Then it was rented as a restaurant,
then, after penny-pinching, it declined
to a fenced off, ramshackle storage shed.

These days the Dairy bustles in the summers:
all sorts in shorts and shades and baseball caps
pick snacks and soda pops, load up on maps,
shop souvenirs or line up to be led,
like you are now, all over Central Park.

"I need this keyring. Where's the ATM?"

"Those kids are cutting in. The nerve of them."

It's too much. Let's get out of this chaotic
crossroads.

The Carousel

Back among the grass and bark
with sunlight-sieving treetops overhead,
we both succumb again to freer forces
than fuss and fluster. After passing under
the candy-stripe-hypnotic, the quixotic,
Playmates Arch, we reach the Carousel,
where fifty-seven gleaming handmade horses
stand poised to orbit straight toward big-eyed wonder.
Go buy a ticket; for a spell, dispel
your darn adulthood. Here the only course is
abandon. Climb astride and grip the pole.

The first iteration of the Carousel, which operated from 1871 to 1924.

The Wurlitzer says "waltz," the platform whirls,
and you go up and down and round and round—
a whoosh stampeding a tableau vivant
of stallions through their constant caracole.
You just keep laughing, and the boys and girls
keep waving at their nanny, mom or dad.
A hooved kaleidoscope of lope and sound!

The revolution winds down, but the jaunt
sustains, beyond that blinged-out helipad,
the breezy high of being nowhere-bound.
Now you are errant. Now you look alive.

The Mall

We step with pep northeast on Center Drive,
then, with a pivot, strut into the round
plaza that feeds the south end of the Mall—
just one of many meditated realms
in the deliberate world of Central Park.

The only trees they let in here are elms,
and lamps in them add romance to the dark
and little shadows when the toothed leaves fall.

The Literary Walk

This southern stretch has lots of statuary.
We don't have time to chat about it all,
but these four—the quartet of literary
celebrities—they'll get a quick roll call:

First Shakespeare, shoulders under robins, grips
a book of verses we will love to quote.
He made the magic of the English tongue
and knows it. So much voltage, so much zing.
Four hundred years, and most of what he wrote
still nightly lightnings from electric lips.

Next Robert Burns, whose tenor lived among
lovers and buddies and the winds that blow.
Think of it: "Auld Lang Syne"—he wrote the thing.
He turned to song when he expired young.

Facing him sits a cordial but metallic
Sir Walter Scott, the Scottish dynamo
who packed rapture into expansive tomes
and hot and harp-like lyrics. All the rage,
he taught grand passions to a bookworm age.

Last our forgotten, lamb-chopped Fitz-Greene Halleck.
Half Yankee Byron, half New York Thoreau,
he penned polite lampoons and nature poems
from the outlook of Appalachia's brow.
So big a star, and no one reads him now.

The Women's Rights Pioneers Monument

After the boys who wassailed, walked and wailed
in rhyme, we pivot and behold a band
of sister suffragettes: the Pioneers
for Women's Rights. It's just a couple years
since this communal sculpture was unveiled.
Let's jump the fence and get the panorama.

Three once molten figures sit or stand
around a table:
First, Sojourner Truth,
who didn't run but walked off in her youth
to freedom. When she sued to bring her son
home from a slaveholder in Alabama,
the case went to the nation's highest court,
and birthright swayed the justices. She won.
Later, she toured the Northeast to exhort
all hands with votes to grant coequal rights
to all.
Across the tabletop from her
Elizabeth Cady Stanton holds a quill
and questions. After battling the slur
of laws insisting Blacks rate less than Whites,
she fought misogyny in Holy Writ.
No doomsdayer or dogmatist could make her
stop proving wrongness with patristic skill.
Nothing could make her mute her mother wit.

Susan B. Anthony stands over them
and heeds and leads. A battle-hardened Quaker,
she spoke to teach the future and condemn
stale sneers. The slow Nineteenth Amendment passed
the tardy House and Senate and at last
was ratified in August, 1920.

Ten decades asked but, though there had been plenty
of monumental men throughout the park,
there still was not one real-life woman cast
in bronze. And so my sculptor-poet friend
Meredith Bergmann poured each matriarch
and poised her in this trio without end
to celebrate the say of womankind.

The Lilac Walk

Pushing beyond the Mall road, which is lined
by elms alone, we pass a ginkgo, turn
northwest near volleyball and soon discern,
behind a scrim of oak and maple trees,
manicured grassland without mud or rock.
The lane that runs along its northeast edge
has started thinning to the Lilac Walk.

First set in motion in the 70s
with foreign futures, Chinese, French and Dutch,
this grove makes stars of what some use as hedge.
A sign of spring, its fragrance is a shock
even in April but by May so much
aroma storms the air that some allege
olfactory ecstasy, wild highs that send
the mind abroad.
                         Here's what I recommend:

go when the day is sunless and the sky lacks
azure so that, beneath a mat of cloud,
your eyes may fully focus on the lilacs'
impertinent flamingo pinks and loud
lavenders. Colors pop out of a pall.
Sad that they turn jejune in June and fall
in fall, but now at least there's no big crowd.

Ah, here it is: the boulder stamped with text
exhorting us, in copper, to recall,
even amid conflicts and confrontations,
"beauty and the lovelier relations
we humans share."

Sheep Meadow

Alright, let's stand here, lurkers
among the lilacs, and admire what's next:

although Sheep Meadow seems a natural lawn
spontaneously apt for lying on
and sharing wine, a picnic or a kiss,
that's not the case. Roughneck destruction-workers
had to blast away a lot of rock
to make these acres run as smooth as this.

Initially a living print to look at,

not tread, this glade exhibited a flock
of sheep—quite countable romantic rams,
quaint wethers, and nostalgic ewes and lambs,
even a shepherd who could shake his crook at
naughty bleaters.
Yes, one wants to fall
asleep in there, but we've got lots to gawk
at waiting.
First we light on a café,
then the expressway switchbacks, and we walk
east toward the teeming zenith of the Mall.
You must not miss out on Bethesda Terrace.

Eagles and Their Prey Statue

Right where our route turns back into the quad
we look up at *The Eagles and Their Prey*,
an all-too-lifelike sculpture cast in Paris:
two huge ones are flapping as they flay
a hunkered baby goat.
Beyond that odd
homage to butchery, the trees are all
elms, elms again, a monoculture. Zero
hawthorns, zero . . .
Hold on, hear that call?
That whistle? That's the eastern meadowlark.
And there he is—a flagrant splotch of yellow—

atop that pole. Look close; he wears a dark
V on his chest like he's a superhero,
"Valentine." It's like the randy fellow
is serenading us as we approach,
humbly on foot, without a steed or coach,
the stately centerpiece of Central Park.

Bethesda Terrace

A saunter through the Tesla-coil-charged air
between Beethoven and the bandshell where
his thoughts come back to life, and we arrive:

Bethesda Terrace runs across two levels.
The upper, aerated by Terrace Drive,
provides the consummation of the Mall.
Vendors and horses hang here. It's a hive
for tourists, but the corbels, pommels, bevels
and trefoils, neo-Something doodads, all
so hifalutinly solicit them
that they don't catch this pair of pillars that
exhibits prime a.m. and grim p.m.

The eastern one is Dawn: a rooster revels
in daybreak, puffs up big to welcome it;
his sleeping cottage wakes to five bound sheaves.

The western one is Night: an owl and bat
adore a contrail witch whose horde is thieves,
goblins and ghosts. A Bible opposite
is lamp-lit, urging talismanic prayer.

Beyond the low wall at the Mall's north end
there is a sapphire circle in a square.

Escorted by cascading balustrade
of Cyclopean thickness, we descend
to the red flagstones of the Esplanade.
All eyes must focus on the fountain where
one of the famed Creator's sterner daughters,
the winged, unworldly Angel of the Waters,
reaches to touch the tap stuff dropped from basin
to basin with the punch of healing powers.
I always wonder if there could be grace in
a hand or ghost in water or a heaven
afterward. I don't know. But who could chasten
the Times of Life, the Seasons and the Hours
for dancing like it's all one deathless jubilee?

The Arcade

Now swivel to the south and check out seven
vaulted ways into the Terrace. Three

run through like subway lines. The air those aisles
are harboring sustains the whole Arcade
and links the Lower Terrace to the Mall.

Echoes are in those hollows. Every wall
is China, and the ceilings are inlaid
with fifteen thousand vintage Minton tiles.
There's so much soothing in ceramic shade.
In August, after roasting on a hike,
you can go there and hide out and get cool
among the murmurings. It shells you like
an empty and upended swimming pool.

The Lake

We see, beyond the Esplanade, a slender
leg of the Lake, a lushly wooded shore,
erratic rowboats and, in all his splendor,
a red-and-white-stripe-shirted gondolier
sculling and steering with a lone long oar.
His two fares, paramour by paramour,
seem to sense Venice in the atmosphere.

The Loeb Boathouse

Toward Queens there, past that willow's supersize
light-grab, the latest Loeb Boathouse supplies
marine cuisine and eager waiters waiting.
Now, in addition to embarking on
the rowboats they have rented by the hour,
people can eat sea bass while contemplating
the creak and plash of human paddle-power
beside the silent saunter of a swan.

After a lull brimful of watching live
lapping against the edges, we resume
our travels, heading west on Terrace Drive.

The original boathouse (1873–1954),
designed by Frederick Olmsted and Calvert Vaux.

Cherry Hill

A side path leads off north, and we have gone
from full sun to the daze of Cherry Hill.
Here, toward the end of March, Yoshinos bloom
hot pink and white and radiate perfume
that smells like almonds taste, and guests arrive
in droves and feast their eyes and breathe their fill.
A good, deep huff, and they are whooshed westbound
across divides and islands, the Date Line,
and meditating in a Shinto shrine.

Still here, we find, on top of rising ground,
a round, redbrick plateau and, at its heart,
a pool whose finial showcases sheer
excess. One chucks modesty to admire
the rings of bling it boasts, tier after tier.
The basin offers up aquatic art.
Water, as animating magnifier,
keeps quickening sheaves, shields and shined profiles
of ol' Abe Lincoln from whatever year,
and every cent is what we most desire.

Way back when way more buggies were for hire,
a hack horse, after trotting many miles
with bale on bridle paths, would trudge up here,
at long last catch his breath and, harness off,
make this extravagance his water trough.

Bow Bridge

Down on the shore beyond the cherry trees
we spot a bypass through the troposphere:
a vault is leaping, with apparent ease,
its own reflection in the earthbound Lake.
(Engineers are like wizards when they make
inert stuff get up and put on a show.)

Bow Bridge, which arches like an archer's bow
and looks like frosting on a wedding cake,
hitches refined and highbrow Cherry Hill
to the rough Ramble. Circles in a chain
make balustrades, and walnut from Brazil
veneers the lengthy walkway, which is titian
on dry days and vermilion in the rain.
And, yes, the view. There is a long tradition
of sweethearts taking sweethearts here to make
the gem-backed ask.
Kudos to those who say,
"I do," but we won't cross their bridge today.
We're sticking to the south side of the Lake.

Wagner Cove

All ears eavesdropping on a duck's admission
of ache and flirting mergansers galore,

we reach a recluse bay called Wagner Cove.
A brief pilgrimage southward down the shore,
and we can see, inside a guardian grove
of willow, cherry, mulberry and oak,
a little lakeside timber-roofed pavilion
inviting us to come sit down and soak
the small things in:
                                        a clawed, then webbed reptilian
limb maneuvering a hull of shell,
a vertigo of pumpkinseed, a yolk
of inky shiner fry; the rocked airbrushes
of water watering. Too much to tell
is in our eyes . . .
                                    I'm glad you chose to try it—
just sitting here and seeing, being quiet.
Remarkable how meditation hushes
not just the larynx but the self as well.

Still open after waking from the spell,
we wonder at the viridescent rushes,
dragonflies and a pink-lace lotus blooming
among the lily pads.

The Daniel Webster Monument

                                        Too bad our journey
along the lakeshore can't sail on forever.

Just past a crossroads, we confront a looming
Daniel Webster. He, some say, was clever
enough to beat the Devil's top attorney.
His free words got to Hell's own jurymen.
He logged eight terms in Congress. Though he never
was president, he tried and tried again.

I understand. Your rolled eyes seem to say:

"So what? Why should the people of today
remember some windbag from way back when?"

Indulge me.
Think of how this bronze remains
unshakeable in every kind of weather—
rainstorms and hailstorms, blizzards, hurricanes.
That's how unshakably the real guy tried
to keep fragile America together
while needing freedom for us all. He died,
then came the War Between the States.
Divided
again, we wait. I hope some slickensided
healer like him can staunch the fault before
the big one and a second civil war.

Strawberry Fields

After we leave the banks where moist sod yields
beneath our feet, we labor up a steep hill
and face a garden called "Strawberry Fields."
Our tour hoped never to attain this scene,
but here we are, and we will see this through.

Look at the flowers, every bloom, bud, sepal;
look at the trees—dogwoods and river birches
from all around the world. Here's what they mean:
America is good at shooting people.
Yes, we are vengeful, we are ill—it's true,
and we must not hush up our annual quota
of massacres at schools, shows, stores and churches.
Here's an example of what a Yank can do:

In 1980, on December 8th,
a person of insane religious faith
followed John Lennon back to the Dakota
and pumped him full of hollow points because
the former Beatle had proclaimed his band
"more popular than Jesus."
So in June
like now, across the street, we get a stand
of blazing yet blasé azaleas,
and struggle-toughened strummers sit and croon
songs like "Imagine" in the afternoon.

To shrive a crime the world will never pardon
America gives prayers and a peace garden.

. . .

Let's go back over all we got today—
the inland seas, the frilled and the no-frills
terrain and doves and that last sad ovation.
None of it grants degrees or pays the bills,
and that's the point: to purposefully stray.
You said, *why not?*, when Big Diversion beckoned,
and we went so far in we got away.

There's recreation and there's re-creation.
You look enlivened: less too tired and more
gung ho; less wallflower, more troubadour.

We stroll out of the park on 72nd,
and off you go into the subway station,
sun-kissed, it seems, less elsewhere than before.

WALK TWO:
For the Fallow

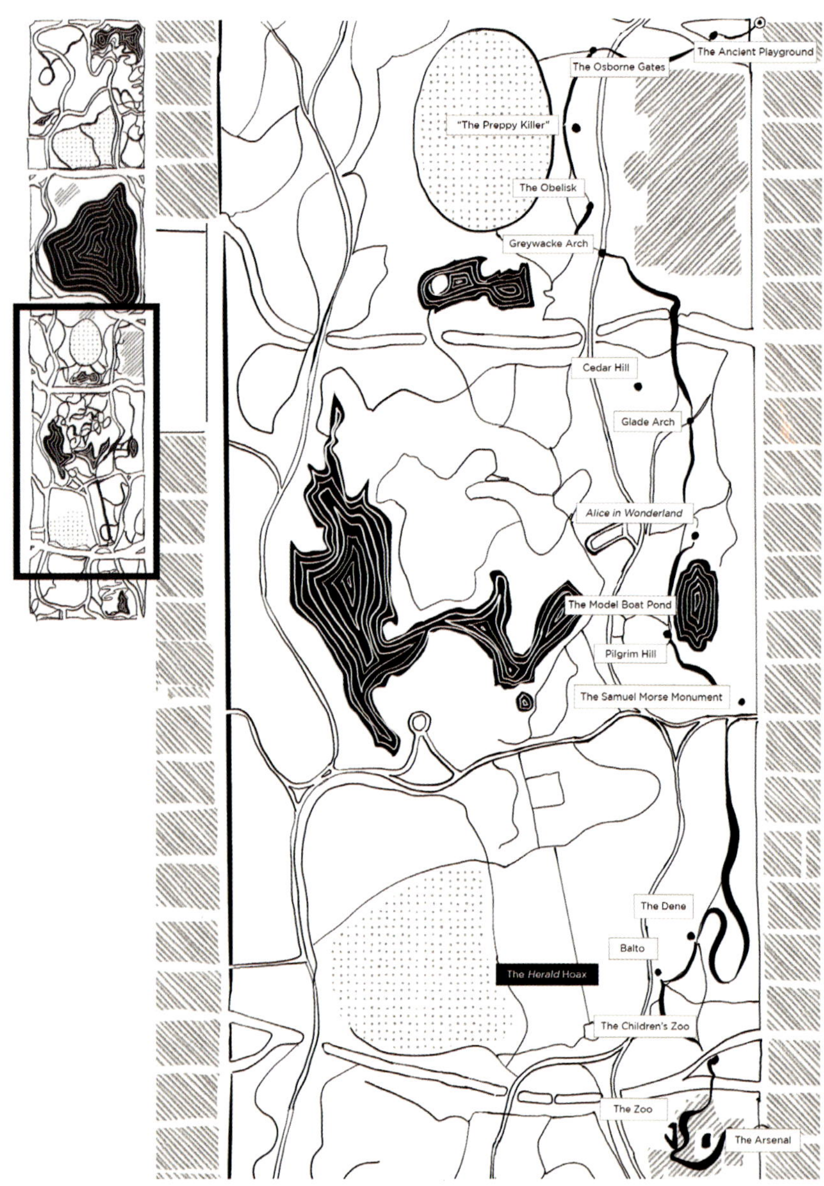

Start: 5th Ave and 64th St

The Children's Gate

Perfect: ice creams and a nice day out.
Today we'll enter through the Children's Gate.
That's right: we'll go on make-believe safari,
pretend a walkabout and laugh and shout
like fascinated children, but (I'm sorry)
this tour's for grownups. Our ambitious route
must pass through omens of our nation's fate,
a hoax and history and homicide.
There will be much to notice, much to mull,
much we agree on, much that will divide.

The Arsenal

Beyond the gate, the westbound walk is focused
on the impersonal, square Arsenal.
Passing beneath hawthorn and honeylocust,
we face two towers, like guards, against its walls.
A stern stoop gathers to a sturdy door,
and past the lintel stacked bronze cannonballs
urge on an eagle armed with angry wings.
Funny, but, never active in a war,
this depot wound up housing other things,
like cops, iguanodons and weathermen.

The Zoo

We hang a right, then hang a right again
and soon are at the entrance to the Zoo.
I flash our tickets; turnstiles go "click-click,"
and hubbub hits us. We maneuver through
a flock of kids agape or chirping, pass
more kids and reach a jungle faced with brick.

"Dad, are there snakes in there?"
"In science class
Ms. Moussa said some monkeys throw their poo."

The Tropic Zone, humectant territory,
displays rainforest on luxuriant levels.
Upstairs, through teleporting plexiglass,
we find ruffed lemurs huddling en masse
or riding rope-swings through the overstory.
Saki monkeys, white-faced little devils,
sleep, leap and nibble mushy pears, while naughty
tamarins, hunched atop a platform, moon
thrilled children.
Downstairs on the jungle floor
we see a ring-tailed western dwarf coati
(a sort of hose-nosed, sausage-shaped raccoon)
just chilling like he's home in Ecuador.

Back in the sun, we walk down larking lanes
to a cascade in a more temperate space
where, fragile in the shallows, white-naped cranes
move, when they move, with ballerina grace.
A shrinking number of these crooners dwell
in the reduced lagoons of Kazakhstan.
Fewer duets are ending up as shell
and yolk and clutch each seedtime.
Pushing on,
we travel east and end up in Japan
where two snow monkeys watch an aunt or mother
teach them the loving way to groom each other.
They learn so fast. Their language is complex.
It even breaks down into dialects.
They get to do what only thumbed ones can
and no harm, too.
Next, lying in the shade
along a granite ledge, a lone snow leopard,
her eyes jade cameos, her white fur peppered
with specks to blend her with a winterscape.
Oh my, she's gorgeous, but there's still a maw
behind the plushness in that ambuscade
and eighteen slashes. Apprehensive awe
says "just keep watching."
After her, we gape
at three bears, grizzlies, from—who knows—Wyoming?
They once had rambling and honeycombing,
but Goldilocks ransacked their robbers' den
and stole the wide West with their precious porridge.

All they can do is ritually forage
about for what they won't get back again.

Although no polar bears are kept here now,
I still remember, in the '90s, how
one of them, poster child, would not stop, day in,
day out, swimming in a figure-eight.
There was less brunt of him at every weigh-in.
It was as if he could abominate
the lot he'd got, could protest, with obsessive
iteration, caged existence.
                                        Gus,
what were you signaling with Sisyphean
insistence? You reminded me of us
Manhattanites and the recursive stress of
running in circles, running round this town.
You did what pent exasperation does.

His brain got tumors so they put him down.

Look here: we love the harbor seals because
they choose to frolic in their tank of brine.
Some don't allow life's confines to confine
their whole existence. Watch them move their slappy
flippers for the joy of it. They live
for happiness and making people happy.
To be a party that you give, give, give—
there couldn't be a lighter-hearted credo.

The penguins strike me as sophisticates,
like in that old song, "Puttin' on the Ritz."
You know it? "Have you seen the well-to-do"
parading "up and down Park Avenue"?
Each of them cliquish, each in a tuxedo,
these chubbies are the gents who, pictures show,
strolled through our streets a hundred years ago
with monocles, watch chains and walking sticks.

Finally, in the center of the Zoo,
there is the mouthwash-blue sea lion pool.
Playing the acrobat or cad or fool,
they storm on stage. What's in their bowl of tricks?
One somersaults against the see-through sides
like an Olympian, while another glides
above the surface, chatting with the world.
Eager, meanwhile, for dainties to be hurled
into his bark, a third one does a dance
that fascinates the family audience.
Now and again a hunk of hake or herring
leaps, and his whiskered muzzle, with unerring
precision, snaps it, spineless, from the air.

The Children's Zoo

After a push through turnstiles, we, a pair
of primates, pass beneath the sandstone leap

of Denesmouth Arch and reach a fairly new
enhancement to the park: the Children's Zoo.
See the suspicious having probatory
experiences by reaching out and petting
cavies, zebu and miniature sheep?
And yet, for all that contact, there've been no
accounts of livestock nipping hands and getting
nasty. And that reminds me of a story.

The *Herald* Hoax

It was a hundred fifty years ago
that ace ink slinger Joseph I. C. Clarke
reported on the front page of the *Herald*
that crazed beasts, vengeful beasts, had gotten loose
from the Menagerie in Central Park:
"Death Carnival!"
The story was profuse
in gore and brio: rampant rhinos barreled
down 5th, impaling businessmen and buskers;
packs of Siberian wolves, grin-faced, made feasts
of pushcart peddlers; lions dined on mothers,
then ate their kids like custards for dessert.
Yes, there were even two disgruntled tuskers
mashing the parasoled. Thus far the beasts
had done in fifty, injured many others.

Panic put all five boroughs on alert.
A chorus of concerned, hardworking folks
aghastly clamored the police chief do
something to fight back, but he knew, he knew,
the whole bombastic bloodbath was a hoax.
The piece had even said it was untrue
way at the end. No one had gotten hurt
or robbed or dead—what charges could he press?
There were true crimes and real-world capers
he had to send his men out to address.

That day the *Herald* sold a lot of papers.

Never fear: the beasts here don't get pert,
let alone lethal. Lambs just can't be scary,
and no one dreads what guinea pigs might do.

The Balto Statue

Wandering northwest from the Children's Zoo,
we push uphill, then idle to assess
a bronze and monumental husky: yes,
a dog. Your furrowed forehead seems to query
what in the world he could have done to merit
this tribute. There's a story, and I'll share it,
a real tearjerker.
Imagine 1925:

Balto, circa 1925.

a plague in an Alaskan January—
diphtheria—and white-outs and subzero
temperatures. No one dared to fly or drive,
and cases just kept mounting. So our hero,
king among canines, was engaged to carry
the vital vials of antitoxin serum
west from Nenana all the way to Nome.
Off he went over vacancies of snow
through nights of night and days of night and gloam.

Momentous voices on the radio
laid out the stakes, and we could only cheer him,
the leader of the fifty-two-pawed team,
onward, onward, to our west most extreme.
We sighed with one breath when the doomed were saved.

And here he is for children to enjoy
and us, who reach like them to pat his gleaming
withers.
You, Balto, were a real good boy.

The Dene

We mush and glide on down an asphalt-paved
ski run that slaloms past primeval-seeming
megaliths installed to make the scene
suggest the heft of Stonehenge. When the Dene
reveals its emerald corridor, we rally
our forces, clamber up a rock formation
and join the slatted shade of the vine-teeming
Summerhouse. Vista greets us, and we scope,
north of us, a Northumbrian re-creation:

styled after, say, some river-chiseled valley
in Thrunton Wood, it's got adrift path streaming
through it, and its left bank, called "The Slope,"
brandishes New York wildflowers and grasses.

Some go for nature, some for artifice,
but this composite landscape more than passes
as both innate and made. I go for this.

We hike down from that latticed bungalow
examining, through polarized sunglasses,
the greens that glisten and the greens that glow.
We come round at a clearing and appraise
a bunker boasting ramps and passageways
open to all, just off Fifth Avenue:

"Hey, I'm a cave-explorer."
"Dad! Yoohoo!
I'm hiding. Get me."
We can hear them laugh
and catcall in the pint-sized labyrinth.

The Samuel Morse Monument

Way east toward 72nd, we admire
a Moses-bearded wiz atop a plinth.
His name is Samuel Morse. He was, of course,
not just inventor of the telegraph,
but coiner of a code of dits and dahs
that, instantaneous, ran along a wire
faster than words can dash on foot or horse.
Without him, we would not have had the phone,
smartphone and all that. So okay: applause.

Pilgrim Hill

Once across Terrace Drive, we leave the stone
pathway and stray together. Passing over
Kentucky bluegrass, dandelions and clover,
we push uphill and find, beneath a stand
of blanched-bubblegum-blossomed cherry trees,
a statue by John Quincy Adams Ward:
a Pilgrim in a buckled steeple hat,
knee-booted, with a musket in his hand;
and, on the base, a Bible and a sword.

As bronze, it's handsome, but there's all of that
violence the Pilgrims thought would please the Lord.
There's all of that inventing adversaries
to turn the faithful to incendiaries
Jonathan Winthrop first, then Cotton Mather,
decreed to be religion.
                                        I would rather
move along.

The Model Boat Pond

                                        We move along and reach
an ovate ocean edged with concrete beach.
We see in it no Puritan Mayflowers,
but pleasure-boats, fun-loving watercraft,

some rigged with mainsails, some with engines aft.
There are a thousand hobbies to enjoy,
a thousand ways to spend unearning hours,
but helming mini vessels seems the most
fanciful and impractical diversion.
Let's stop and look at this chaotic toy
armada—call it Spanish, call it Persian,
call it the mess of ships that sailed to Troy.

Steerspersons standing all around the coast
are holding short-range radio remotes
with which they pilot peewee motorboats
and (frequently becalmed) wind-powered yachts
through circular excursions. There are races
on Sundays, and engrossed supporters cheer
on runs that top out at a couple knots.

Nothing of note could ever happen here—
that's why it's one of my most favorite places.
So much of life is trifles. Come some day
when you are burnt and overburdened, rent
a sailboat at that shipyard tipped with steeple—
the Kerbs Boathouse—and join the other people
idling a summer afternoon away
as sailors tugging on remote mainsheets.

The Alice in Wonderland Statue

Landlubbers ambling between cement
seashore and oak (the shipwright's tree), we wend
north till we greet the Empress of Pretend.

As if at home enthroned atop the cap
of a bronze mushroom, Alice sits and greets
the ribboned kitten climbing up her lap.
Around them stand the zanies who inhabit
Wonderland: the be-Wellingtoned Mad Hatter,
pocket-watch-harassed White Rabbit
and dozy Dormouse. Their unending chatter,
no doubt, is rich nonsense, rich innocence.

This piece wants you to join it, so don't stay
back there like an observer sitting on
a "real" park bench pressed against the fence.
Go walk among the wonders, climb and play.
Go live a life of curious events.

We spend a spell atop the Helicon
of Daydreams, breathe what Alice has to teach,
then head on north.

Glade Arch

Once we have made our way
past sycamore and hornbeam, birch and beech,
in full midsummer greenery, we reach
the beige Glade Arch. We push through and are gray
inside a monumental crescent moon
of shade that simultaneously regards
one's batting record and one's next at bat,
tricks won and lost and what is in the cards,
shows that have closed and features coming soon.

Cedar Hill

Just past that span, a northern habitat:
pines, spruces, cedars—lucky evergreens
not doomed to end their days as Christmas trees
or lie, post-Christmas, in the lumberyards.
Resin aroma blizzards Cedar Hill.

Even in summer I see winter scenes
when looking up there, like it's ten degrees,
but exercise is cooking off the chill:
a top-like saucer or dead-on toboggan,
bouncing down the staggered outcrops, ends
up scattering a free-for-all of friends
with snowballs destined for a chest or noggin.

Chaos is not a game that one can win.

Yeah, even on a hot day we're right there,
sweating out warmth beneath our wool long johns,
plaid flannel shirts and parkas trimmed with fur,
as we perfect a snowman. *Make his hair*
pine needles and his eyes dimes. Make the grin
a bit of fraying bootlace.
Bodied in
brief stuff that melts at lower temps than bronze,
he always dwindled inly to a blur.

Greywacke Arch

But that's behind us. Past the grove that keeps
its tines forever, trees that shed a load
of leaves in autumn—oak, elm, ash—recur.
Two in a crowd, we cross a bridge that leaps
eternal traffic on the Transverse Road.
Then, brushing past the cypress-garnished green
that runs along the south side of the Met,
we trend northwest and, idling between
sycamore maple and a sycamore,
look up at Greywacke Arch.
We've seen a ton
of spans, but this is an exotic one:
peaked like an entrance to a minaret,

the arch evokes Moroccan Mogador
or something out of Saracenic Spain.

When did the Moors take the Americas?
Sometimes it seems like all that ever was
is in Manhattan. What would we leave for?
We've got this park.

The Obelisk

We take an asphalt lane
due north and reach, among magnolias,
a dolmen that demands a big description.

Oh, America! What have you done?
Why drag the huge thing over? Just because?

Three and a half millennia this Egyptian
boast has been around. The hieroglyphics
heap Ozymandias with honorifics
such as "Ra's Chosen One," "Son of the Sun,"
"Giver of Life" and "Treasure of Osiris."
His victories, too epic for papyrus,
insisted on the lastingness of granite.
Quarried near the Nile, the thing was shipped
from Alexandria's Caesareum
past Crete and Malta halfway round the planet

to the East River. Then a herd of horses
dragged it out here.
                This dominion-tipped
insistence that our country has become,
you know, like, one of history's great forces
nags also no one reigns eternally.

TURNING THE OBELISK.

Plate XXVII a

“The Preppy Killer”

Proceeding north through mostly elm, we see
a rare black maple and a back-packed birder
with opera glasses studying a—what?—
a cedar waxwing in a redbud tree.
And that’s the very spot. I’m sorry, but
we have to stop and talk. There was a murder.

August the 25th of ’86
was sunshine and an optimistic breeze.
“Papa Don’t Preach” was tearing up the charts.
Light beer was hot, coke was the favorite fix,
and yuppies made purée with Cusinarts.
In toy stores, Care Bears reigned, and fashion fads
exalted *Top Gun* Ray-Bans, crop-top tees,
and power suits bulked up with shoulder pads.
The Dow kept climbing while, in politics,
Reagan was selling missiles to Iran
and Gorbachev was furthering his plan
to make the backward factories of the vast
USSR more profitably run.
Capitalism, it would seem, had won.

That night a flawless nineteen-year-old hunk
who’d gone to prep schools in his bad-boy past
stopped in at Dorrian’s (a vast saloon
at 84th and 2nd) and got drunk

with an eighteen-year-old. Her dreamlike swoon
got worse with every round. They left at last
and strolled into the park to get it on.

But what a bicyclist found here at dawn
was scratched and savaged body. It was she—
two weeks from college—right beneath that tree.
Detectives whistled over the details.
Snarled clothing lay around her on the lawn.
Her throat was purple. Then the fingernails:
blue bruises underneath them seemed to say
that, as she died, she tried to pry away
the double clutch of her assailant, lover—
whatever fiend had choked a life out of her.

During the time the CSIs were working,
her beau, still easy on the eyes despite
the scratches to his face, was still there lurking
behind some bushes. Then he snuck off back
to his apartment.
When the cops arrived,
he vowed his cat had clawed him in the night.
He'd met that girl, but he'd gone home to bed,
and she'd gone off alone to buy a pack
of cigarettes. When the detective said,
"She didn't smoke," he backed up and contrived
the tale that he would milk: the so-called "victim"
had started choking *him*. She had gone mad.

He had fought back, and she had not survived.

There was no way that she could contradict him.

Down at the precinct, just before his dashing
mugshot was snapped, he shouted to his dad
the chick was crazed and wouldn't let him be.

Straightaway daily papers started splashing
alluring pictures of "The Preppy Killer"
above the fold on every front page. He
was all the rage. The Mideast shrank to filler.

In court his lawyer, got at great expense,
contended she, an alcohol-dependent,
insistent little chit, the brazen daughter
of money, had been forcing the defendant;
he only strangled her in self-defense.
Nine days the jury was deliberating;
nine days the tabloid hacks were salivating—
and then he copped to first-degree manslaughter.
The sentence: fifteen years. He served them all.

Though there's no shrine or marker to recall
Jennifer Levin, testaments abide.
Landscapes can flashback. When you pass this place,
the honey locusts and lone sawtooth oak
that witnessed murder always will evoke

her final evening, his relentless face
and horror, horror.
                                        No more homicide.
Let's home in solely on the present tense
and end the day with light stuff. It would be, um,
better, you know, much better for morale.

The Ancient Playground

Skirting the north side of the big Museum,
we reach a final welcoming locale.
It's raucous. From outside the iron fence
we catch the badinage of boys and girls
and reprimands from nannies, moms and teachers.

The Osborn Gates here, fringed with ornaments
like little apples and opposing squirrels,
are worlds where morals are, where Aesop's creatures
parley: hare and tortoise, crow and fox,
mix each beneath a worldly-wise inscription.

Beyond those scenes, Manhattan turns Egyptian:
a streetside playground peaked with pyramids
and Ra's old gnomon. Heck, it even features
dunes for tombs inside a wooden box.

Let's sit here for a bit and slip like kids

into a timelessness of wild what-ifs.
That pool's Nile and that terrier a pharaoh.
And why not names that mean like hieroglyphs?
"Simoom" for me; for you, the quiet one,
"The Sphinx." And now beside the Great Sand Sea
the teleporting sort of levity
is caravanning through us to our marrow.

That's transatlantic and a day well done.

. . .

Just think how much came out of what we saw—
exotic beasts imported to inhabit
coops among us cramped Manhattanites,
then languid sailboats and the rushed White Rabbit.
Ramses the Second's high, old self-hurrah
proclaimed dominion to the unconcern
of geese and picnickers. May all those sights,
like compost and a soaking rain, help turn
your private plot into a bumper crop.

You wanted something, and the park is wide.
We'll meet tomorrow on the other side,
the Natural History Museum stop.

INTERLUDE: A Secret

When I was just a baby in Manhattan
forever running from a mind abuzz
with bumblebees of doubt and wasps of debt,
and all I had was I loved reading Latin,
I wandered round the park behind the Met,
then sat, legs crossed, among magnolias.
Next month? Next year? Mistrust was all there was.
If New York City were a competition
to take some trophy, then I wasn't winning.

So, to forget the brisk, brusque, brutal race,
I started mumble-reading the beginning
of Vergil's *Georgics* in a smirched edition:
Quid faciat laetas segetes—
a fertile little koan meaning both
"What makes plants happy?" and "What makes plants thrive?"

That time exhilaration, like ignition,
sprang from the phonemes. Pigment came alive,

and glee was in the leaves and undergrowth.
The whole unanimous yet multifold
wonderland seemed to need its story told.

Nothing's been funner than my inner oath
to make a garden of that revelation,
to do in our own English what was done
in Latin out of love for Central Park.
Wherever this goes started with that spark.

The whole way home that evening, I was one
among the effervescent vegetation.

WALK THREE:
For the Melancholy

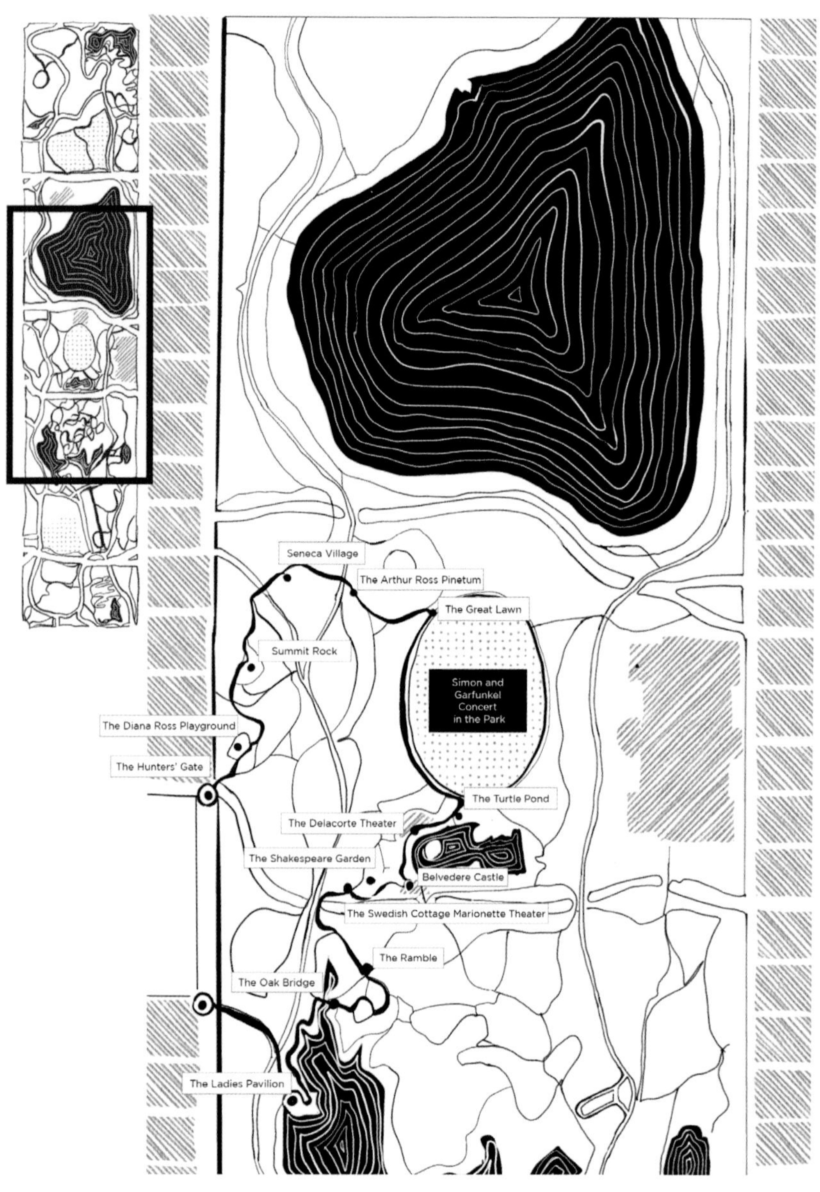

Start: Central Park West and 81st Street

The Hunters' Gate

The blocks end after traffic lights and straight
acceleration. At the Hunters' Gate
a clubhouse rule kicks in: it's mandatory
we aim for something as we make our way
off-grid through fields and groves. That's right: today
we'll both be hunters and, with any luck,
secure our quota of a skittish quarry.
Sorry: we won't be scrutinizing muck
for tracks toed toward New York Bigfoot's address.
Nope, we'll just hope to stumble on our prey:
flash Inspiration and surprise Delight.
They're great when got and rarely dangerous.
Now put them from your mind because, the less
we go for them, the more they'll come to us,
and straight to us, the more that we digress.
Not hunting them—that's how you hunt them right.

The Diana Ross Playground

Just round the corner, we absorb good cheer:
a wild playground, uproarious, named after
Diana Ross. Prolific always, she
reigned from the record down to the CD
and gave a fortune.
                    What a romp lives here:

emitting singsong taunts and hee-haw laughter,
the gang is hanging from the monkey bars
and riding spirals to the desert floor.

They've clearly found what we've been looking for.
Their gripes and grudges, though, don't cling like ours.
I've got a hunch we'll need more than a spree
of acrobatics and ecstatic talk
to treat your case of fully grown ennui.
Come on, we'll find the cure. Let's go explore
the south slope of that monster Summit Rock.

Summit Rock

Aches in our calves, hamstrings and derrieres,
we don't stop; step by step, we fight the steep.
Each inch feels like a foot; each lift, a leap,
until, at last, the cant and coarse stone stairs
ascend no further. We have earned the crest.

North, east and south display, in singles, pairs
and thickets, lavish tree-life. Sorry, you
would have to fly up as a drone or bird
to get your longed-for panoramic view.
There's this, though: if you turn and look due west
between the cherry trees down 83rd,
you thread the needle and can glimpse a sliver

of Jersey's Hudson Pointe across the river.

Turning to face our "mountain's" southern spur,
we see a rough-hewn amphitheater
laid out to put up traveling sorts of shows.
Beyond it lies a ruminative lawn.
I know it's tempting—azure-eyed repose
for hours, but we must keep moving on.

Seneca Village

After descending, we confront West Drive,
stop short to reckon with the traffic flow,
then, as in Frogger, risk it and arrive
at what at first seems just a grove of cherry,
buckeye, oak and hawthorn. Did you know
that way back, *ante bellum*, in this very
spot was a village? Now there's trunks and rocks.

A little Irish and a little German,
but mostly free-state Black, the run of blocks
accommodated multistory houses.
It was a 'burb before there were the 'burbs.
There was no cramp up here or stench or vermin—
none of the darting filth that still disturbs
downtowners. Workmen with their kids and spouses,
after sleeping in and putting on

their Sunday best, would go to hear a sermon,
say, where that dandelion is today.

Us sitting here is why that ward is gone.
Commissioners with eminent domain
bought out the landowners to pave the way
for this abscondment known as "Central Park."
Real homes were razed to house synthetic wonder.

The Pinetum

After adventuring through groves off-lane
and clambering up mossy outcrops under
scattered shadow, we must cross the stark
sunlight that warms West Drive. Then, getting clear
of ginkgos, elms and oaks, familiar trees,
we reach the round Pinetum. Let's stop here
and take the whole centripetal display in.

Look at them, lean and leafless. Pines, pines, pines—
guests like the Austrian, Swiss, Japanese,
Korean, Mexican and Himalayan;
natives with names like Weymouth, pitch and limber.

The Greeks grew just this sort of prickly timber
in consecrated spaces, plein-air shrines
that honored Bacchus and the goat god Pan.

It would be nice to be a clergyman
urging observance of the evergreens.

The Great Lawn

We make a quick jog south beneath the cover
of spiky species from the whole world over
and reach one of the big park's biggest "scenes:"
the wall-to-wall Great Lawn, a perfect place
for people-watching, playing fetch with Rover,
kicking a ball or spooning with a lover.
And there's a pair in a risqué embrace.
Focusing on the squirrels, we make our way
along the grassland's west side—mostly oaks.

There's just so much behind some fields we see.
When I walk here, a way-back memory
from elsewhere starts replaying:

while my folks
would always, after pancake breakfast, play
Simon and Garfunkel in Central Park
on Sunday mornings, it was getting dark
here in September, 1981.
Song after song, from "Mrs. Robinson"
down to the encore "Sound of Silence," Simon,
strumming guitar and singing lead, would carry
the melody, and Garfunkel would chime in

The Concert in Central Park, Paul Simon and Art Garfunkel, Rainer Halama

with those angelic harmonies of his.
People (a half mil) whooped; the band was "on;"
and we, off in the North Dakota prairie,
were carried years away to this Great Lawn
in New York City.
                    Memory is crazy:
what *was* right here and *was* back there still *is*
right here because of back there. By some mazy
logic, that album worked like destiny.
And they are still replaying—an unseen
mirage.

The Turtle Pond

West of that well-mowed oval, we
meet oaks and willow oaks and, not too far

beyond them, squint into the tints of green
that mean the Turtle Pond. At first, we see
just reeds and algae blooms, then there they are:
painted and snapping turtles, red-eared sliders,
some surfacing, some rocklike on the rocks,
some on a slo-mo hunt for water striders.
Many of those out there were pets before,
the kind a kid keeps in a cardboard box
until his parents say the little guy
will have to go back home. That "home" is here.
After a solemn ritual on the shore,
they tilt and tilt until *Kersplash!* Goodbye.

Dark-watered though it is, the Pond reflects
an oval sky encroached on by the sheer
excelsior of turrets on a bluff.
You point to ask: "What's that? Some kind of fort?"
It's special, and we'll storm it soon enough.

The Delacorte Theater

We push on west then stop to pay respects
behind the platform at the Delacorte,
where anyone can watch the best dramatic
literature ever scripted come alive
for free. I said this park is democratic.
All that you do for tickets is arrive

at 8 a.m. the morning of the show
and stand in line a bit. Then find a date
or grab a friend and, close to sunset, go
and claim your seats. They're all up near the stage.

Everyone, even the completely broke,
can watch the greatest actors of our age
entice as Cleopatra, rail as Kate
and roar the mad home truths of King Lear's rage.
Here Patrick Stewart in a heat wave donned
a Prospero in rags, no cap, no cloak,
and worked some magic while that castle's towers
joined in above the coolness off the Pond.
Antsy New Yorkers hushed for two full hours.

Belvedere Castle

Making our way along the shore, we pass
willows and cypresses, lake-loving trees.
The grass keeps giving way to more and more
boulders and outcrops, then we face a mass
as daunting as Denali. No more ease,
my friend. We were just warming up before.

We take a steep slope to the park's top floor,
pass over ramparts made of Courtly Love
and Disneyland, then touch Belvedere Castle.

All local shist, it seems to grow out of
the grayish Vista Rock it stands above—
a natural bastion.
                                        Each an eager vassal
of the commanding spectacle, we gape
north at the Great Lawn and the Turtle Pond.
So green and groomed and grand, and then, beyond
the trees' reach, crenelated cityscape.

We have to wonder, with the build-up hike
behind us and this view before us, like:

What should we make of this contraption? This
thesaurus of Linnaean nomenclature?
What should we make of manufactured "Nature"?
Of large-scale truly fruited artifice?

Belvedere Castle, Central Park, N.Y, from Robert N. Dennis collection of stereoscopic views

What should we make of this communal ark
of chocolate twists, chipmunks, and high romance?
This charged terrarium of choice and chance?

There are so many shades of Central Park.

The Shakespeare Garden

We come down from that gallant precipice,
then wind a short ways west and, passing through
a modest sort of gateway marked by yew,
enter the Shakespeare Garden.
                                        Though "a rose
by any other name would smell as sweet,"
Linnaeus loses us in clarity
that only means as far as Latin goes.
Familiar nomers keep the most drift neat.

Meandering among the species, we
alight on pink, five-petaled eglantine,
just made for garnishing a hat or line
of lilting poesy. Bed by bed, we come
to holly branches ending in a burst
of crimson that insists it's Christmastime;
columbine whose capri-and-teal bells chime
with sky and tree-top shimmer; primrose, first

celebutante of spring; and marjoram,
the badge of harvesttime and happiness.

But there are glum plants, too; there's the bouquet
for other days. This garden must confess
wormwood, the oomph of absinthe, which, they say,
turns us to trembling delirium;
rosemary "for remembrance," which in vase
or hand calls up the casualties of war;
and cyanotic rue, "sour herb of grace"—
repelling bugs is what it's most used for.
Strange that, just sitting pretty like decor,
those herbs mean toxins, losses and liqueur.

The Swedish Cottage Marionette Theater

A hop-skip past that postlapsarian Eden,
and we have reached the next treat.
Built in Sweden
and shipped here for our first World's Fair, the pine
Cottage now hosts a puppet theater.
The door is open and admitting stray
latecomers to the daily matinee.
We follow, sit and gather, line by line,
the tale the agile-trebled puppeteers

are making playthings paint in pantomime
is "Sleeping Beauty:"
Once upon a time
a pretty princess pricked by fairy malice
was doomed to sleep the sleep of untold years
until a true love's kiss awoke her. Well,
many a suitor visited the palace,
kissed her and failed, but then one day a prince
kissed her and with his true love broke the spell,
and so they lived happily ever after.

Now Perfect Rightness dances to convince
our doubts it lives, and we applaud, and now,
each fastened to a handler on a rafter,
the dolls that have convinced us take a bow.

The Ramble

Sorry to quit that credulous abode,
we trek southwest through yew trees. Once we cross
the nameless bridge that hops the Transverse Road,
hazel and hackberry are letting less
light through, and all is labyrinth and loss
of where the sun will set. Now we must guess
or, better, live with circling through the scent
of worm-dank earth, because we're in the Ramble.

After decades of mismanagement
it turned more canopy than undergrowth.
The scant scrub left was all crabgrass and bramble.
Balanced out now, its wilds abound in both
brushwood and cover.
                                        Who'd have thought the great
metropolis' depths would look so rural?
It's like we've gone and warped somewhere upstate.
The paved lanes splitting into dirt paths trailing
off into *Where the Wild Things Are* feel neural.
Whichever road you go down, there you are—
facing yourself in every rendezvous
with what's out there beyond the wooden railing.

Sapsuckers rasping through their repertoire
profess malaise. An owl inquires, "Tu-who?"
and silence is the answer of a town
millions of voices strong.
                                        If days here skew
Jungian toward "the shadow," then the nights
are Freud's "libido." Once the sun goes down,
cruisers come out to hook up with who's cruising.
All heights and sizes, bodies of one's choosing,
foregather under few and feeble lights.
Over a hundred years the punctual rhythm
of their abrupt affairs has made this zone
notorious.
                    I've got no problem with them.

Why wait around forever? Why behave?

We mount a rise and face heaped blocks of stone
that for a hundred years have sealed a cave,
the Ramble Cave now secretly renowned
for suicides.
                    Way back, inside the grotto's
echoes, one drew a gun and turned it round
and ended what he'd tried. The note they found
was eloquently brief: *My name is boy.*
No family in this country. There are mottos
for desperation; then there's that envoi.

Still worse, atop those steps, another one
flicked out a razor meant to shave a face.
After a nod of farewell to the sun,
he cut too low. He vented with the spout:
"One of the sparrows told me I should do it."

Go on, groundskeepers, plant more phlox and bluet;
you can't blot out the past that owns this place.

Now that we've roused the discontented forces,
hauntings are everywhere, and we want out.
Lighting at last on sun and lakeshore, sources
of sure intelligence, we make our way
over the Oak Bridge over Bank Rock Bay.
We have survived the Ramble.

No more doubt
will dim today's excursion.

Balcony Bridge

Following
a thoroughfare that skirts the Lake's west side,
we pass row boats, then promenade across
the asphalt-paved yet quatrefoil-refined
Balcony Bridge. One feels an urge to fling
one's tenor at the lovers drifting by.
The peach tree and the joyance and the toss
of water—everything is saying "sing."

The Ladies Pavilion

A quick trek south along a wide path lined
as much by cliffs of leaves as clefts of sky,
and we trend shoreward and discern, behind
a scrim of London planes and coffeetrees,
redbuds and rhododendrons, the ornate
Ladies Pavilion.
Look what's going on:
pastel hydrangeas and anemones
array a runway running to a bride

View of Ladies Pavilion looking south. West side of Lake, 1984

whose skin is gleaming, every milkmaid plait
is gleaming, and her layered dress, chiffon,
is geyser. She alone is deified
until another bride, with cadent gait
(and what must be her father at her side),
starts down the path in tux and cummerbund.

After the yearning eulogies of singers,
a flight of rings alights on left ringfingers.
A kiss says, "Yes," and then two laughing packs
of bridesmaids scrum to catch the two bouquets.

. . .

Stuffed with juvescence and the whole new fund
of visions we have met at every height,

we hike northwest and, up a little ways,
survey a bridge that couples two vaults' backs.
Our walk across it in the late-day haze
feels like some old initiation rite.

We've passed: two seekers, each a neophyte,
now grasp how sightseeing assuages sorrow.

New York, New York has never looked so bright,
and there will be still more to see tomorrow.

WALK FOUR
For the Disillusioned

Start: Central Park West and 106th St

The Strangers' Gate

We've seen so much; we need to see the rest.
I know: three days of gallivanting through
the park with me have asked a lot of you,
but think of all that's out there. Time to rally.
Cascades and wilds await.
                                        Before us stands
the Strangers' Gate, which faces, to the west,
what realtors have dubbed "Manhattan Valley."
East of it stone stairs step up to our quest.

Do you like traveling to foreign lands?
You know how, when you first arrive abroad
and see a town you've never seen before,
everything fascinates: a church façade,
a tent bazaar, even a sketchy alley?
All of our senses, presto, notice more.
That's how I hope you'll gaze upon the various
attractions we'll be visiting today.
We keep best what we see the stranger's way.

The Children's Glade

The staircase tops out, and a gentler grade
uplifts the green stage of the Children's Glade.

Its current denizens include gregarious
geese, two birders and a wet-grass breeze.

But actors come some days, then families
convene, lean back on stone and watch a play
in which a pipsqueak, say, takes down a giant.
Once here I saw a lakelike dance recital
spawn true human swans—no pantomime.
But what I like the most is story time.
The ones that we remember teach how vital
immersion is and, if a mind stays pliant,
wonder can be worked on every tale.

The Great Hill

We push on east through elms some yards off-trail,
then crest the Great Hill. Swiveling, we stare,
through gaps in the surrounding foliage,
south, east and north at Central Park expanding
in greens or blues and at the West Side where
thick-grown apartments, an expensive hedge,
conceal the Hudson and the Palisades.
But no more brick and steel. We're here for shades
of viridescence.
A sustained break standing
amid the jade, and we are off again.

The trees grow closer, and the breezes cool.
Hawthorn and ash are reaching toward us, then,
behind a Herculean sycamore,
we face the pipe-fed lake they call the Pool—
a green lagoon, a sluice, a tarn. We turn
and mosey east along the root-wreathed shore.
Hearing, ahead, the permanent applause
of water as its drops, we soon discern
a tiered cascade.

Glen Span Arch

A jag downhill between
forsythia and hickory, and we pause
to take in Glen Span Arch. Beneath it run
both the main path that wanders the Ravine
and the endearing brook they call the Loch,
which burbles from the Pool toward Harlem Meer.
Quarried from Fordham gneiss, a local rock,
the bridge's rough-hewn ranks of stone appear
as natural as all else in the scene.
The vault transports us to a Roman bath
whose vines are timeless.

The Ravine

Once inside the canyon,
we trend northeast along a sunless path
and cross a raw, anonymous stump bridge.
The Loch has faded to a hushed companion
but still consoles, with devious good cheer,
Manhattan's bleakest wilderness frontier.

So many trees. The whole northwestern ridge
is densely trunked and shaded: river birch
and willow, black, red, white and swamp white oak.
They'd rather be alone. When deep in here,
I catch the vast, like, panoramic fear
of wilderness oblivion. No joke.
The sun goes out. Then, after rangers search
weeks for us during sudden Arctic weather,
do we get found? Do we rub sticks together
to win back warmth and signal them with smoke?

Still worse, the light and lornness here evoke
a desperate Dante. Hiking up a slope
as vastly overgrown as that, he found
wild beasts so mean he wound up giving ground,
panicking and abandoning all hope
he could do anything but detour, enter
Hell and confront the Devil at the center.
He went so far to come back from the dead.

RUSTIC BRIDGE AND CASCADE IN RAVINE.

We've got it good. I mean, who could despair
beside a cute stream with a bridge ahead?

Huddlestone Arch

Huddlestone Arch was built years back to bear
foot traffic, bicyclists and carriages
over what mucks up shoes and tires. It is
a sight to feel—those boulders pressing boulders

down with crushing poundage. We beholders
marvel at, under all that mass, mere air.
Physics, you are a miracle! Just think:
those crude unwieldy Cyclopean stones
were made to float by heft, tension and sweat,
and all to save a silly rivulet
that trickles from the Pool to Lasker Rink.
A drip outweighing ten-ton brunt!

Go on,

since everyone is pulling out their phones
and taking pictures, you should take some, too.

Lasker Rink

When you're full-up, we push north, passing through
azaleas and crowds and sweeps of lawn.
Blue tile has started inching into view.
We pause politely as a grande dame schlepps
her purse and poodle down a run of steps,
then get dropped off at, like, a giant sink
brimming with teal degreaser.

Lasker Rink,

right now in summer, is a swimming pool.
Adults do laps; kids go to swimming school.
And now the bronze lifeguard has blown her whistle.
At whom? At us? That speedo-sporting stocky
guy who forgot to "walk instead of run."

When snow falls, all this ocean turns to ice,
and figure skaters come. Thugs come for hockey.
Walloping a round, hard-rubber missile
past Jason-facemasked goalies can be fun.
The sport is less a game and more a vice,
but padding up like some Homeric grunt
in helm and greaves and battering the brunt
of armored others in an hour-long war
once meant, for me, what winter was about.

The Harlem Meer

Proceeding north past warblers in a stand
of locust trees, we meet the southern shore
of Harlem Meer, a modest lake poured out
back in the 1860s to erase
marshy, mosquito-breeding bottomland.
Its shoreline now is lively civic space
on warm days.
We'll be back here to explore
this fourteen-acre focal point some more,
if we escape, intact, the desultory
wild across the way. For now at least
check out Duck Island, sovereign, to the east,
peopled by pitch pine and a London plane.

The North Woods

East Drive behind us, instant overstory
starts shining darkness on what seems a lane.
Mysterious inside the inner city,
the North Woods, acres of amok, contain
much that's seductive, much that isn't pretty,
and there is outrage at the heart of things.

"The Central Park Five"

It's like the specter of a grisly sight
has turned that oak grove grim. The wrong still stings.
The trauma-tripwired spot should wear a shrine
that names the many victims.

                                        Though the night
of April 19th, 1989,
was calm at first, just after 9 p.m.
a teen battalion crossed the borderline
from grid to park. What had got into them?
All whim, no qualm, they started whipping rocks
at carriages then, spoiling for a fight,
went on to beat up those just taking walks,
riding their bikes or sitting in the dark.
The ERs filled with wounds.

                                        Still worse, that night
a jogger was discovered in the park,

right where those oaks were sprouting leaves, off-trail.
Cops shook their heads at how she had been bound
in cord and left not there. A doctor found
the DNA of one offending male.

The coma meant she was sometime a blank,
but then her family named her: Trisha Meili,
associate at an investment bank.
All that the doctors gave her to entice
her eyes to open failed to raise her from
the ocean floor. A priest arrived to give
the deathbed unction and viaticum.
Nobody thought that she was going to live.
She came back all the same, but she came back
with not one moment of that night to plumb.

The cops had started dragging suspect teens
and all the pals they named down to the station.
Many were Hispanic; most were Black.
After intransigent interrogation,
lies like threats and smacks behind-the-scenes,
five wearily confessed on video tape.

Inevitable guilt was taking shape.
The DNA meant nothing. Though the sample
recovered was a match to none of them,
confessions gave the DA more than ample
assurance. Cloven into staggered trials,

the five wore suits while being implicated
and sat on what they could have said *pro se*.
Attorneys spieled; jurors deliberated,
then "guilty," and they all were locked away,
one as an adult, four as juveniles,
each for the maximum the law allowed.

However veritably they avowed
their innocence, presumption made them stay
unheeded. When the youngest four were out,
the eldest by the oddest chance one day
uncovered more than reasonable doubt:
a fellow con confided, "It was me."
A month before a mouth swab could confirm
the lifer's guilt, and then the fifth went free
eleven and a half years through his term.

The five accepted as a settlement
millions to buy out all the life they'd spent
in cells, but who can estimate the cost
of personal freedom after it's been lost?
Two of them champion changes to prevent
others from getting locked up like they were.

And Trisha Meili. What became of her?
She went back to her job, went back to running
and published *Hope and Possibility*,
a guide that coaches wounded souls still shunning

the often violent world of outside things
through reemergence to recovery.

The trees reach out to snag us. There's no fence.
We breathe air charged with chirrs and flutterings.
It is the brood less often seen than heard.
For instance, that cascading breathy trill
means bobolink and that's a whippoorwill.
Hear how exuberantly he laments
his lonesomeness? The pitches really carry,
and then surprise: the silence afterward.
Soon, on the far side of a hushed suspense,
a dark-eyed junco in a forked black cherry
starts lavishing a tintinnabulary
toccata on his backwoods audience.

There's so much concert time when you're a bird.
Think of it: music is their art *and* speech.
Though what they say may be out of our reach,
the pitches still mean things and make great sense
as shots at beauty.
                              So, with little throats
in tree-tops warbling motifs with moxie,
we amble westward through the woods until
we spot a sandstone bunker on a hill,
a steep one, so we make like mountain goats.

The Blockhouse

Although us Yankees reared this squat and boxy
blockhouse for the War of 1812,
them Brits had built the podium years before
during the Revolutionary War.
I love that one. Indulge me as we delve
into our dawning.
                                    First Sir William Howe
came marching in through what is Brooklyn now
with musketeers and Hessian mercenaries
to put our pesky insurrection down.
Then came their "wooden wall:" instead of ferries,
sightseeing cruisers or a garbage scow,
square-rigger frigates loyal to the crown
were bobbing in the Hudson.
                                                  Here it stood:
a battery of cannons that could flatten
uprisings from us trodden snakes downtown.
Redcoats were marching through my neighborhood!
Imagine: subjects reigning in Manhattan.
Monarchy, frankly, makes me want to puke.
(Strange that King James the Second, once the Duke
of York, is why we live in "New York City.")

I like to light off fireworks, and I love
democracy, but ours is failing fast.
Our future threatens to become our past.

That's all the moral I can squeeze out of
the stone foundations of this hunched, unpretty,
like, Lego building.
                                        We descend and start
making our way back east toward open park.
There's so much forest everywhere, above
our heads, on every side, each tree like art
a curator has poised there for appraisal:
a birch with pianola-paper bark,
a buff-trunked maple living hand-in-glove
with knitted ivy, and petite witch hazel
whose each branch-end is a divining wand.

The Lily Pond

We reach the switchgrass where the Lily Pond
once rippled. Nope, there's no more font, no fish
and not one single penny for a wish.
It tried to be a sight that eyes would visit,
tried for years and failed, and now what is it?
This rampant situation where it died.
A sad, sad void, but let's get out of here.

The Discovery Center

Once we have crossed East Drive and left the wild,
some sunlight-buttered gaps of grass appear.
Squinting again, but seeing far and wide,
we stroll along the north shore of the Meer
until we meet a "Little Women"–styled,
two-story house with bright-red A-frame gables.
That's the Discovery Center.
                                        Once inside,
we move through cooler air and wall-to-wall
inquirers studying displays and labels.
Here, with an ID, you can rent the stuff
you need to play old Roman bocce ball
and Old Norse kubb. Also, if young enough,
you can check out a bobbered rod and fish
(catch-and-release) the Harlem Meer's north shore.
There, if remissly dreamy, you might see,
among the panpipe reeds and mermaidish
nitella, miry make-believe and more—
everything lakeside reverie divines.

Here also are some plaques and plastic signs
that tell the story of geology.
Come, let us learn about our lithosphere:

Back in an eon known as the Taconic,
torrid infernal temperatures and chthonic

travail transformed the sea's lees stranded here
to marble, schist and gneiss—bedrock with ridges
that stick out of the dirt. A bunch of bridges
we've crossed are made of just those sorts of stone
so that they look at home, less made than grown.
And we've seen upthrusts from the park's foundations
peeking above where they were squeezed together.
Remember Summit Rock and Vista Rock
that wears the castle? Aged by endless weather
and scored by ice and lovers' declarations,
they sure have character.
                                        It's hard to talk
in here with all the battling orations.
Let's step outside . . .
                                        What a release it is
to hear a hush again. I know: my mouth
is yapping yet, but someone has to be
the docent as we tour this gallery.

After some neo-Gothic cypresses,
we amble east a while, then swivel south
and stroll on down the far shore of the Meer.
It's kind of spooky quiet over here.
We meet no stroller-traffic-jams, in stark
contrast to all we braved back round the bend.
No trot of Percherons; no whoosh of bikes.
New York, for now, is you and me, my friend.

The Bernard Family Playground

We pass the smallest playground in the park
(meant for the littlest of the little tykes).
No one is squeaking on the swings today,
no one exulting in the constant spray
shot from the fountain. But there still are trees.

You smell that honey? That's a flowering linden.
The old wives use its spores to sweeten teas.
Over there near the shore, that weeping willow
both lifts one's gaze and drops it. Watch the wind in
its lithe Rapunzel tresses; watch them billow
and settle, billow, settle. Soothing, yes?
Though desolate, these acres are as rich
as real uncultivated wilderness.

The Conservatory Garden

Passing between custodial oaks, we enter
the posh Conservatory Garden which
exhibits three distinctive national styles:
here on the north side, the fastidious French;
symmetrical Italian in the center;
tousled English to the south.

Our sneakers
go drifting inward through concentric aisles.
Passing the hush of fellow pleasure-seekers
side by side or solo on a bench,
we weave through curved shrubs groomed to look like lawns.
They ring the fountain ringed in by the bronze
Three Dancing Maidens. Hand in hand, the girls
saltate and circle as the jet unfurls
élan between them.
Look how art can thrive.
If we ran splashing through and joined them there—
still lives, we would forever be alive
the breathless way ecstatic artworks live.

Leaving the spheres of that *système solaire,*
we cross into a quad evocative
of dons and doges: promenades, a lawn
restrained on all four sides by well-clipped yew.
This is the lordly sort of Xanadu.

A geyser iridescent as chiffon
soars and subsides as mist between two rows
of rainberry. The pergola that stands
behind it wears wisteria which, in May,
ripens to purples, mauves and indigoes.
West of it one big sycamore commands
a steep escarpment.

Every Saturday
in summer rented limos named "Just Married"
pull up and park on Fifth, and brides and grooms,
whole wedding parties, strut in here and pose
for pictures. I have never tied the knot,
but Paolo and Francesca would have tarried
to touch, sigh, kiss and more in such a spot
(if they had not gone young to separate tombs).
So, yeah, love fits in here. I understand.

The final paradise, if not as grand,
is shaggier, more spontaneous, more varied.
Flowers abound here, brilliant beds of blooms
for every season. (Now, in June, it's phlox,
peonies, baby's breath and hollyhocks.)
Here also, in what seems an arbitrary
arrangement, trees give refuge from the sun.
For me, they conjure up a legendary
English forest, Sherwood, say, or Arden,
where good guys, temporarily on the run,
reclaim what's theirs, and wicked kings regret
their wickedness.
The statues in the pool
commemorate in art Frances Burnett,
who wrote the children's book *The Secret Garden*:
a girl's hands heft a birdbath, while a boy
plays flute forever. At their feet, a school
of sunburst-red and rainbow-colored koi

Statue of Mary and Dickon from Frances Hodgson Burnett's "The Secret Garden" at the reflecting pool
the Conservatory Garden in Central Park, New York City, by Carol M. Highsmit

idles at random under lotus flowers
and lily pads. We could, of course, spend hours
idling here (that's what it's for), but we
have miles to go and butterflies to see.

Exiting England, we proceed though oaks
and lilacs, oaks and lindens, then arrive
at a stop sign and chockablock East Drive.
A panting pack of bicyclists goes by,
their pedals blurred, their wheels paired blurs of spokes.
We cross lit pavement under open sky.
Then, after trekking through a hawthorn-hazy
swatch of grass, we reach the little sector
of Central Park that's all about the nectar.

The Butterfly Garden

Blazing Turk's cap, snow-white Shasta daisy,
sun-loving aster, toothed chrysanthemum
and latex-weeping milkweed drive them crazy—
not just the hummingbirds and honeybees,
I mean the stained-glass monarch, pied pearl crescent,
speckled sootywing and iridescent
painted lady. They can't help but come
and with their tubular embouchements tease
sweets from the stamen where the pollen is.
Watching them flutter on prismatic wings
and flash among the flowers, one must concede
they are the gaudy gods and goddesses
of all "come-hither" creatures, all bright things.
It just makes sense: eye-candy that they are,
sugar is all the nourishment they need.

The North Meadow

Setting out south, then, from that glam retreat
to start the long trek to the Reservoir,
we pass, wide-eyed, through elm- and maple-shadow
but stop and switch to squinting when we meet
the batting-caged and canvas-based North Meadow.

One can only marvel at the torque

with which a hypertrophic handgrip whips
a wad of cowhide-cushioned yarn and cork.
Then come mitt-slap or the cathartic crack
of ball on bat. And, Oh, that Yogi Berra
is genius with his witty little quips.
The smartest aleck of the Wise-Guy Era,
he taught philosophy while talking smack.

You hear "A nickel just ain't worth a dime"
and "gets late early," but this off-the-cuff
query of his does not get posed enough:

"How can we think and hit at the same time?"

You know, the world is out there chucking stuff
our way, and there's that choice to be unwary
and go to greet it or sit back and eye
its possibilities as they pass by.

The Reservoir

We look both ways and cross the Transverse Road.
After a hike down through the musk of cherry
and piquant rush of bluegrass getting mowed,
we reach the joggers on the Running Track
that cuts a route around the Reservoir.
The shoreline, like their sneakers, circles back.

Excuse the patter, but I can't help touting
this vista's virtues. First admire the star:
the Floating Fountain like a whale is spouting
out there, eclipsing Rockefeller Center.
But, wait, there's more—a whole gabbling rabble
resides here. Look, a bright-browed bufflehead,
a preening grebe, a loon (the sweet lamenter),
and wood ducks—both a white-eyed hen and randy,
red-eyed drake. They come to build a bed
among the rank, mud-rooted reeds and dabble
in the protected shallows. March through May,
the cherries blossom here like cotton candy.
Plus, just look at it: who could be stressed
with all that water sauntering that way?

The Gothic Bridge

Skirting the shore fence widdershins, we meet
the clockwise joggers running two abreast,
in tandem ranks, at random and alone.
But we're here walking. We walk past the stone
Pump House and stone Gate House (both obsolete)
and crest the Gothic Bridge, a steel-gray span
with trefoil tracery. Let's take a rest
atop it and survey the traffic.

Serving

the Running Track and walkways to the west,
this leap comes out of the original plan.
Under it runs the dirt-paved Bridle Path
where leaves heap up in autumn and unswerving
joggers and trekkers face the foulmouthed wrath
of carriage drivers, who have right of way.
The world needs rules, it seems. What can I say?
Meeting demands with interlocking layers,
the park's complex but, as a whole, makes sense.

The Tennis Center

A dogleg down a zigzag path back north,
and we are clinging to a chain-link fence.
Beyond it, there are pairs of tennis players—
the guys in pleated shorts and polo shirts;
the girls in polo shirts and pleated skirts.
Everywhere back and forth and back and forth,
off clay, off rackets, up and over nets.
Hard not to follow as assertive servers
and fleet receivers charge through games and sets,
through matches, gracefully. As mere observers,
of course, we'll never get to "live" the sport.

Look at the pro there teaching how to swing.
She winds up, bumps the orbs, and they all carom

off anywhere she sends them in the court,
while newbies, scattering them harum-scarum
everywhere but in bounds, keep practicing.
It's like athletics and the arts are kin.
Tough years of polishing technique go in
to effortlessness in the end, we hope.

The Safari Playground

After transecting, to the west, a ring
of hawthorn, elm and pine, we cross West Drive.
The waiting pathway climbs a clement slope
past Chinese scholar tree (a stock shade-giver
at Buddhist shrines) and ornamental cherry.
Then, passing under oak leaves, we arrive
at the Safari Playground, where a blue
meandering mat and sloshing splash pad carry
imagination to the Congo River:

a dozen life-size hippopotamuses
lumber and slog about, some half immersed.
A small one smiles beside a green canoe.
Another, possibly a baby brother,
nudges the rump of what must be his mother,
while papa, gullet gaping, offers us his
most extravagentest yawp, a burst
of five-ton thunder.

Fresh from orange buses,
red wheelbarrows and their parents' hips,
preschoolers shout amid the tame stone bloat.
Rope-netting feels the pinch of little grips;
wee feet negotiate the wood step climbers.
Moms cheer and giggle, and a few old-timers
chuckle and nod. Their bodies are afloat
on dry land; everyone has given way
to the deliverance of all-out play.

. . .

Four walks to conjure what had been dispelled
have taught us promontories, what a boat
conveys to eyes, the brick, baroque and burly
bridges, and countless quiet ways to stray.
We glugged abundance as the sources welled.

Here we are, truants, but tomorrow early
you will get back into the quick-trade biz,
scrutinize odds and trends, then mind the Dow.

Thank you for sharing sights and silences
with me. I know how wonder disappears
and hope our travels stick with you for years.
Keep coming out for fresh adventures now.

EPILOGUE:
The Vista

No clouds today, no blot about since dawn,
just periwinkle over where I'm sitting,
cross-legged, toward the center of the Lawn.
While Tai Chi bends and breathes, frisbees are flitting,
as pink and lime blurs, in and out of view,
and three stray soccer games are going on.

The bluegrass blazes hints of royal blue,
and, from the margins, rain-gun sprinklers shoot
life-giving salvos as if to salute
Belvedere Castle's vista in the distance.

That sense of a utopian existence
alive inside our own is coming through.

Those of us who get drained by what we do
need trusty getaways like Central Park
to brim ourselves in. We need lake and lark.
Everyone, everyone, deserves escape
from gridlock, glitches, cubicles, red tape.

A zone of unrestraint within the tension,
a healthy folly, a resort dimension—
if a good rain of liquid Happiness
could fall on landscapes, they would turn to this.

Central Park in Literature

Central Park is not just a place; it is a myth. Though many books and guides present, some in minuscule detail, its geography, flora and fauna, there has not yet been anything that focuses on what the park means to the imagination, America and humanity. That is the purpose of this excursion. We will move chronologically through portrayals of the park in prose and poetry. Though not comprehensive, this survey aspires to be inclusive. Illustrious novels by F. Scott Fitzgerald and J. D. Salinger and high-brow nonfiction by Henry James will have to endure rubbing shoulders with children's literature, song lyrics, and pulp. A democratic approach is fitting: as the park welcomes all comers, this essay should encompass all kinds of literature.

We will see the park in different seasons and visit a range of attractions. Not surprisingly, the Zoo (originally the "Menagerie") has been the most popular subject, but the Boat Pond is a close second, with one character, the miniature Stuart Little, even giving us the pleasure of racing across it in a model boat. Over and over again, the park will "teleport" characters and readers to locales as disparate as Vietnam and Iowa. Reactions to it will range from enthusiasm and admiration to fear and eventually pass into nostalgia not only for childhood experiences there but by-gone eras.

Let's start with the worst: William McGonagall (1825-1902) was an infamously bad poet. Critics assailed him with savage reviews and audiences assailed him with rotten vegetables. What endears him to me is his absolute certainty that he was meant to be a poet and his dogged pursuit of recognition. What's more, as someone who has received his share of rejections, I admire that, for better or worse, he was immune to discouragement and showed insuppressible resilience. In 1878, after his letter requesting royal patronage was rebuffed with a perfunctory "thank you for your interest," he was so certain the response had been favorable that he hiked sixty miles from Dundee, Scotland, to Balmoral Castle, over mountains and through a thunderstorm, to give a reading as the "Queen's Poet" for Queen Victoria. Turned away at the door, he walked home and kept on writing. Since, it would seem, any royalty would do, he took an honorific from a letter in which the "King of Burmah" dubbed him "Sir William Topaz McGonagall, Knight of the White Elephant, Burmah." Though the letter was obviously specious, McGonagall used the title for the rest of his career.

Broke in 1887, he sailed to New York City to seek his fortunes. Hence came his enthusiastic "Jottings of New York: A Descriptive Poem," eighteen lines of which describe Central Park. It is fitting that he visits it on "the Sabbath Day." As we will see, Sundays are especially popular, both in literature and life, for junkets through the park:

And as for Central Park, it is lovely to be seen,

Especially in the summer season when its shrubberies and trees are green;

And the Burns' statue is there to be seen,

Surrounded by trees, on the beautiful sward so green;

Also Shakespeare and Sir Walter Scott,

Which by Englishmen and Scotchmen will ne'er be forgot.

There the people on the Sabbath-day in thousands resort,
All loud, in conversation and searching for sport,
Some of them viewing the menagerie of wild beasts there,
And also beautiful black swans, I do declare.

Say what you will about McGonagall's poetry, the guy wrote what he saw. Rather than present a stop-by-stop account of his visit, however, he groups the material according to theme and its importance to him. The first stanza focuses on the Literary Walk at the south end of the Mall. A proud Scotsman, he gives us the Scottish Robert Burns and Sir Walter Scott, with Shakespeare thrown in for good measure. The fourth writer in the Literary Walk, the American Fitz-Greene Halleck, is utterly neglected, as if unworthy of mention.

The second stanza focuses on Sunday visitors to the park arriving "in thousands," which, nineteenth century century sources suggest, is an accurate rather than hyperbolic estimation. He likely is watching them enter through the Children's Gate (5th Avenue and 64th Street) because he goes on to mention the Menagerie which at the time was housed behind the Arsenal, at the site of the present Zoo. The New York Public Library preserves a late-1900s stereograph of two black swans which very well may be the pair that McGonagall mentions.

And there's beautiful boats to be seen there,
And the joyous shouts of the children do rend the air,

The black swans, Central Park, N.Y,
from Robert N. Dennis collection of stereoscopic views

While the boats sail along with them o'er Lohengrin
Lake,
And the fare is five cents for children and adults ten is
all they take.
And there's also summer-house shades and merry-go-
rounds,
And with the merry laughter of the children the Park
resounds
During the livelong Sabbath day,
Enjoying the merry-go-round play.

The third stanza exalts the Lake, the first of the park's features to be made open to the public (1858). Boats-for-rent became available there in the 1860s, and McGonagall preserves not just the excited shouts issuing from them but, in a bathetic lapse, the exact cost of boat rental for children and adults, as if he were writing promotional copy. The bathos is all the more striking in that, in the preceding line, he, with the lofty literary allusion "Lohengrin Lake," compares the rowboats with the children in them to the swan-drawn boat of Lohengrin, "the Knight of the Swan," a German Arthurian hero who sails across a lake to rescue Elsa, Duchess of Brabant. In the final stanza, he refers to the first iteration of the Carousel, which operated from 1871 to 1924. To make it go round, a blind mule and a horse in an underground trench would trudge in a circle, starting and stopping in obedience to a tap of the operator's foot.

What McGonagall lacks as a poet he makes up for as an enthusiast for all he sees and as a historical source. I can't help but love him. Thank goodness that, after his visit to the New World, he at last found steady work: he recited his poetry at a circus in Scotland. For fifteen shillings per night, he would face a constant barrage of eggs, herrings and stale bread from the audience. Who says you can't make a living as a poet?

Stephen Crane's *Maggie: A Girl of the Streets* (1896) is a great and very depressing novel. It contrasts the squalid and seemingly inescapable Bowery neighborhood with affluent and enticing locales elsewhere in Manhattan. Maggie, who remains naïve a good long while despite her alcoholic and abusive parents and the jaded characters around her in the Bowery, eventually falls for a bartender named Pete, who strikes her as worldly wise: "Swaggering Pete loomed like a golden sun to Maggie." Early in their relationship he takes her to a freak show: "she contemplated [the freaks'] deformities with awe and thought them a sort of chosen tribe." Later on, after "raking his brains for amusement," Pete discovers the Central Park Menagerie, located outside of his home turf, the Bowery, in the Upper East Side. While Maggie "giggled in glee" at the animals there,

> *Pete went into a trance of admiration before the spectacle of a very small monkey threatening to thrash a cageful because one of them had pulled his tail and he had not wheeled about quickly enough to discover*

who did it. Ever after Pete knew that monkey by sight and winked at him, trying to induce him to fight with other and larger monkeys.

Pete sees himself and other denizens of the Bowery in that "very small" but belligerent monkey. We meet Pete as a "lad with a chronic sneer" already at the age of sixteen. He rescues Maggie's brother Jimmie, "a very little boy," from a crowd of other boys who are attacking him. During their assault they emit "notes of joy like songs of triumphant savagery." The monkey evokes a Bowery-style admiration in Pete because, when insulted, it fights every other monkey around until it gains satisfaction. He sees the monkey as having self-respect, as standing up for itself. His wink at the monkey is a gesture of understanding. Like some other primates, the boys in the Bowery are tribal and, when they fight, primitive. As we will see, Central Park in general and the Zoo in particular will often be portrayed as a primeval and savage place. This will not be the last work of literature in which characters see themselves in the monkeys at the Zoo.

Pete and Maggie visit the original Menagerie, which was along 5th Avenue at 64th Street. Founded in 1859, it initially received donations of animals, and the first monkey arrived there in 1860. Roughly two and a half million people visited it in 1873. In the 1880s the Monkey House attracted such distinguished guests as former President Grant, while the city's Irish population objected that names like "Mike Crowley" given to the simians were an ethnic slur. Crane portrays Maggie and her family and friends as Irish immigrants, and Pete himself likely is as well.

In the 1890s wealthy New Yorkers who lived near the Menagerie pressured city planners to move it elsewhere in the park. Though the larger Bronx Zoo was created in 1897 as a result, the Central Park Zoo stayed pretty much where it was. After a period of decline, renovated and expanded facilities for it opened in 1934. After another period of decline, the current iteration of the Zoo opened in 1988, and it is thriving today. Now we will do an abrupt about-face from Pete and Maggie's cramped and narrow Bowery to the airy expansiveness of Henry James (1843-1916).

James writes affectionately of Central Park in *The American Scene*, a collection of nonfiction travel pieces written in 1905–1906. A native New Yorker, he relocated to England as a young man. In this piece, he is oddly both stranger and native. He sees the country where he was born with both American and foreign eyes. Lavish with affection for Central Park, he asserts that visitors instinctually give it the benefit of the doubt, finding it "amiable" because this is "the only way to play the game in fairness." It is there to be loved, and everyone feels an urge to react to it with fondness.

In "Chapter IV: New York Social Notes," the Park is long-suffering and resilient: "The perception comes quickly, in New York, of the singular and beautiful but almost crushing mission that has been laid, as an effect of time, upon this limited territory, which has risen to the occasion, from the first, so consistently and bravely." James has seen vast European parks and gardens like Versailles (twice the size of Central Park), so he sees its territory as "limited." What's more, he exaggerates the smallness of it (a "mere narrow oblong, much too narrow and very much too short") in order magnify "the difficulty" of what it must do. He goes on to personify the park as the hostess of the only inn in town. As we will see, the park and its attractions, when personified, are women.

Since, in James' view, Central Park alone in New York City satisfies "the aesthetic appetite,"

The Mall, 1910

> *The place has therefore borne the brunt of many a peremptory call, acting out year after year the character of the cheerful, capable, bustling, even if overworked, hostess of the one inn, somewhere, who has to take all the travel, who is often at her wits' end to know how to deal with it, but who, none the less, has, for the honour of the house, never once failed of hospitality.*

James continues the "appetite" metaphor by calling visitors to the park "famished" for beauty and romance.

> *It has had to have something for everybody, since everybody arrives famished; it has had to multiply itself to extravagance, to pathetic little efforts of exaggeration and deception, to be, breathlessly, everywhere and everything at once, and produce on the spot the particular romantic object demanded: lake or river or cataract, wild woodland or teeming garden, boundless vista or bosky nook, noble eminence or smiling valley. It has had to have feature at any price . . .*

Whereas other authors compare the park to "Nature," James hints at its artificiality, partly by using cliché Romantic-period diction such as "cataract" (for waterfall), "bosky" and "noble" to describe it. The park even stoops to "pathetic little efforts of exaggeration and deception" in order to provide "the particular romantic object demanded." According to James, its duty is to speak democratically to everyone. That's what makes it quintessentially American. In his view, it must, like a circus or cyclorama, pander to visitors with cheap effects. The implication: everyone's aesthetic assessments are valid. James contends that, just as he hears a smattering of languages spoken by visitors to the park, it is itself "polyglot," communicating something to the fourth-generation New Yorker, the first-generation immigrant and the weekend tourist. To James, the park is versatile, unflagging and eager to please. Whereas he describes abundance "in May and June," our next author gives us bleakness in the middle of winter.

In her poem "Central Park at Dusk," first published in 1917, Sara Teasdale (1884–1933) does not describe the park in detail but focuses on the interplay between the buildings outside of it and the trees within it at what must have been an early, an afternoon, sunset:

Buildings above the leafless trees
Loom high as castles in a dream,

While one by one the lamps come out
To thread the twilight with a gleam.

There is no sign of leaf or bud,
A hush is over everything—

Silent as women wait for love,

The world is waiting for the spring.

A native of St. Louis, Missouri, Teasdale sees the buildings that stand on all sides of the park as "castles in a dream." Though this image may come off as sentimental and cliché, I understand it, and I accept it. I, too, saw these buildings as "castles in a dream" when, a native North Dakotan, I first moved to New York. The castles "loom," however, complicating the image. They are aloof, even intimidating, reveries. We will often see the park contrasted with the buildings that surround it. Private, domestic and exclusive, they conveniently throw its public, plein-air and all-embracing spaciousness into high relief.

When Teasdale mentions the lamps turning on for the night, she is most likely referring to electric streetlamps, introduced to New York City in 1880. The "leafless trees," along with the absence of any "sign of leaf or bud," evoke an emphatically barren scene. The "hush" that she describes, the hush that is "over everything," is distinctly hibernal. Silence can be different in the different seasons. In winter, it is often sad and desolate, as if the whole place one happens to be is itself frozen. Teasdale then compares this hibernal hush to the silence of women waiting for love, and the poem turns yearningly amorous. Impatience and frustration are not only in their silence, but in the park's hush as well. Will spring come at last? It will. Will the lovers come at last? They will. The restless barrenness of the poem calls up future voluptuousness.

In a further surprising turn, the park becomes the "world" in the last line. Given the comparison to women waiting for lovers, the park is feminine, and spring, it follows, is masculine. We end with the suggestion of a future elemental *hieros gamos*, or "sacred marriage," of sky god and earth goddess, vividly described by Homer in the *Iliad*, when Zeus and Hera make love. Finally, given the year the poem was published (1917), I suspect that, when Teasdale wrote "the world is waiting," she may have meant not only "for the spring" in a literal sense but also for the end of World War I, which dragged on until November, 1918. Then at last the war-wives "waiting for love" would be reunited with their husbands. In contrast to the bleak hibernation we encounter in this poem, our next writer gives us, at first, an explosion of color and activity.

Evelyn Scott (1893–1963) was a prominent American literary figure in the 1920s and '30s. Though she wrote often of New Orleans and the South in general, she is not usually grouped with the "Southern writers," but with Modernists like James Joyce and T. S. Eliot because her work was published in the same literary journals as theirs. She is best known for her trilogy of novels, *The Narrow House* (1921), *Narcissus* (1922) and *The Golden Door* (1925) but was a prolific poet as well.

The first half of her poem "Autumn Dusk in Central Park" (1920) presents all the vividness of an expressionistic painting, while the second half, outside the park on Fifth Avenue, gives us, in contrast, dinginess and austerity:

Featureless people glide with dim motion through a quivering blue silver;
Boats merge with the bronze-gold welters about their keels.
The trees float upward in gray and green flames.
Clouds, swans, boats, trees, all gliding up a hillside
After some gray old women who lift their gaunt forms
From falling shrouds of leaves.

Bow Bridge, featured in the Central Park Valentine's Manual, 1868

Thin fingered twigs clutch darkly at nothing.
Crackling skeletons shine.
Along the smutted horizon of Fifth Avenue
The hooded houses watch heavily
With oily gold eyes.

The initial setting, with the people gliding through the water and the wake of the boats, is the Lake, an attraction that also struck McGonagall's fancy. The lateral movement of the first two lines gives way to upward movement in the next two, with the bright "clouds, swans, boats, trees, all gliding up a hillside" toward a drab anticlimax: "gray old women" making their way through fallen leaves.

Shadowy is where the poem stays. As the sun goes down and the perspective moves out of the park to 5th Avenue, "a smutted horizon" populated by "hooded houses" presents itself. The houses are further personified with "oily gold eyes" that "watch heavily." The poem is pure description—there are no emotion-words like "joyous" or "sorrowful" to telegraph how the various images should be taken. It is most concerned with portraying the contrasts between public and private space and between active participation and passive observation.

The lightness and dynamism of the opening three long lines end up leaping outside of grammar as a fragment in lines 4–6. To mark the contrast to the opening, Scott gives us abrupt complete sentences in lines 7–8 and consistently shorter lines, in which the almost leafless trees become "crackling skeletons." Whereas the gliding people in the park are a blur ("featureless") of activity, the static house has distinctive "gold eyes," which "watch heavily." The eyes are "oily," which operates not only in the literal sense but in the sense of "unpleasantly smooth and ingratiating." The houses, with their dour gentility, seem envious of the scintillating exuberance they see in the park.

Jarring and stark, the movement from bright activity to the dark and static buildings outside it enacts the "dusk" in the poem's title. Indeed, after the palette of colors in the first stanza ("blue silver," "bronze-gold," "gray and green"), all that the second stanza gives us for color is "gold" for the houses' eyes, suggestive of affluence.

Affluence pervades F. Scott Fitzgerald's classic novel *The Great Gatsby* (1925). The focus is on the nouveau-riche Gatsby and the old-money Buchanans in the Roaring Twenties. The narrator Nick Carraway, not rich himself, is studying finance. Though the settings outside of Manhattan are semi-fictional, Fitzgerald refers to specific streets and locations when his characters go to the city. Early in the novel, Nick, Tom Buchanan and Tom's lover Myrtle take the train in from Long Island. As if anticipating that the afternoon will turn drunken and ugly, Nick tries to leave just after seeing the park from a cab: "We drove over to Fifth Avenue, so warm and soft, almost pastoral, on the summer Sunday afternoon that I wouldn't have been surprised to see a great flock of white sheep turn the corner." Like McGonagall, Nick is contemplating the park on a Sunday. Though he is on Fifth Avenue, which runs along its east side, his description evokes Sheep Meadow, which is on the west side of the park between 66th and 69th Streets.

A flock of sheep did actually graze there, under the protection of a shepherd, at the time Fitzgerald was writing *Gatsby* in the '20s. They were evicted to Prospect Park in 1934. Tom refuses to allow Nick to leave the party in pursuit of sheep and tranquility, and, in stark contrast to the aforementioned image of pastoral innocence, a bender ensues in which Tom punches Myrtle on the nose and leaves her "bleeding fluently." The park often, as it does for Nick here, evokes a "simpler time," before the world was corrupted, before some felt a need for Prohibition. As we will see, the flipside of this conception is the park as a "primitive" space unrefined by taboos, laws and customs, a place outside of the social contract where savage acts occur.

Later in the novel, Nick happens to meet his love-interest, the golf pro Jordan Baker, at the tea garden in the famed Plaza Hotel, just south of the park. When they go on a romantic evening drive along and through it "in a victoria" (a horse-drawn, four-wheeled, doorless open carriage), Fitzgerald provides vivid local details:

> *The sun had gone down behind the tall apartments of the movie stars in the West Fifties and the clear voices of little girls, already gathered like crickets on the grass, rose through the hot twilight . . . It was dark now and as we dipped under a little bridge, I put my arm around Jordan's golden shoulder and drew her to me . . . We passed a barrier of dark trees, and then the*

facade of Fifty-ninth Street, a block of delicate pale light, beamed down into the Park.

When it marks the southern border of the park, 59th Street is also called Central Park South. Nick's right: the facades of the buildings there facing the park (including that of the Plaza) are, to this day, impressive, especially when lit up at night. The bridge Nick and Jordan pass under before the implied make-out session is most likely the Dipway Arch, which spanned the Bridle Path (for horses and buggies) until 1934. The passage, with its "hot twilight," gives us the park as a setting for romance. That romance also shows up in our next work, along with a feeling of irresponsibility.

Dorothy Parker (1893–1967) was a versatile writer. At times a poet, screenwriter, critic and wit, she famously was involved in initiating the daily meetings of the group known as "The Algonquin Round Table" in 1919. The circle, including such figures as Noël Coward and Harpo Marx, met regularly until 1929. When the group broke up, she moved to Hollywood where she became an award-winning screenwriter and lyricist. Later, blacklisted as a Communist, she moved back to New York City.

She wrote her poem "Observation" in 1925, when she was in her early thirties and lunching regularly with literary luminaries and other celebrities at the Algonquin Hotel:

If I don't drive around the park,
I'm pretty sure to make my mark.
If I'm in bed each night by ten,
I may get back my looks again,
If I abstain from fun and such,
I'll probably amount to much,

But I shall stay the way I am,

Because I do not give a damn.

In this poem Central Park is a folly, a temptation, a distraction that threatens to prevent an ambitious person from becoming successful. Associated with a drive around the park, implicitly, are staying up late and indulging in "fun and such." Everybody wants to be attractive and "amount to much," but few are willing to insist on "beauty sleep" by going to bed early every night. The work-life balance can be especially precarious for artists in that they need time off from work (active creation) to gather material for a next sculpture, painting or dance.

I do not believe Parker when she says "I do not give a damn" about making a mark and amounting to much. Her stubborn insistence on staying the way she is, on taking a late drive around the park and having fun, strikes me instead as a devoted artist's resolution to have a life outside the daily grind of creation, both for her own sake and the sake of her work. In keeping with the romance the park exudes in Fitzgerald's novel and Parker's poem, our next specimen, song lyrics, gives us pairs of lovers sitting side by side on benches there, at the onset of autumn.

In 1934, five years after the Great Crash on Black Tuesday, most middle-class New Yorkers were living paycheck to paycheck, and shantytowns for the homeless, named "Hoovervilles" (after President Hoover), were burgeoning in Central Park. That was the year the songwriter Vernon Duke (1903–1969) composed the music and lyrics for "Autumn in New York," a jazz standard that has been recorded by many artists.

The concluding lines wind up in the park:

The gleaming rooftops at sundown

Autumn in New York

It lifts you up when you're run down

Jaded roués

And gay divorcees

Who lunch at the Ritz

Will tell you that it's

Divine

It's autumn in New York

Transforms the slums into Mayfair

Autumn in New York

You'll need no castle in Spain

Lovers that bless the dark

On benches in Central Park

Greet autumn in New York;

It's good to live it again.

Given the poverty and starvation going on all over the nation at the time it was composed, this song is willfully escapist. With lots of leisure time because of unemployment, Americans did, in fact, turn to escapist fiction, such as comic strips, comic books, and pulp fiction, in the 1930s. Songwriters also wrote lighthearted songs to distract their radio and concert hall audiences from the Great Depression. So, here, instead of homeless people in soup lines, we find "Jaded roués / And gay divorcees / Who lunch at the Ritz." To them, life is "divine." "Slums" are mentioned, but only to be transformed into a presumably floribund Mayfair Market in England. "You'll need no castle in Spain" really does seem to mean that the people living in New York slums would prefer to go on living in them rather than move to a castle in Spain because New York autumns are beautiful.

The song ends with the image of "lovers" sitting "on benches in Central Park." Why do they "bless the dark"? Why do they "greet autumn in New York"? "Bless" is not being used here in the priestly sense but as an expression of gratitude, as in the phrase, "Bless you for doing that." The lovers are grateful for the dark, it would seem, because it is where they are comfortable being physically intimate. They greet autumn because there will be more "lights out" time. Enough with the adult situations now. Our next work will bring us back to an age before we cared about mooshy stuff like that.

E. B. White's children's book *Stuart Little* (1945) is a classic of the genre. The protagonist, Stuart, is remarkable: just over two-inches tall and a mouse, he lives in a comfortable domestic situation as part of a family. He is precociously articulate and resourceful for a six-year-old (and for a mouse). His best friend is a songbird Margalo and, when two cats who are plotting to eat her drive her away, he goes on a quest to find her. Before the quest, however, Stuart has a one-day adventure in Central Park.

When he arrives at the Model Boat Pond, White vividly describes the boats and their shore-bound captains in a time before motors and radio remote controls were available: "The owners, boys and grown men, raced around the cement shores hoping to arrive at the other side in time to keep the boats from bumping." After selecting the *Wasp*, "a big, black schooner flying the American flag," over the other boats, Stuart explains to the owner that he is "looking for a berth on a good ship" and eventually "signs on" to race another boat that has always beaten the *Wasp* in the past. Stuart, in a sense, "teleports" from the Pond to an ocean. "Teleportation," that is, the leap from a present setting to an evoked setting through imagination, is common in literary accounts of the park. Again and again, attractions in it will be gateways to faraway places and other times.

Just before the start of the race, White describes the behavior of the New Yorkers who have gathered round to watch:

> *When the people of Central Park learned that one of the toy sailboats was being steered by a mouse in a sailor suit, they all came running. Soon the shores of the pond were so crowded that a policeman was sent from headquarters to announce that everybody would have to stop pushing, but nobody did. People in New York like to push each other.*

New Yorkers do have a reputation for being pushier than Americans elsewhere. I have lived all over the lower forty-eight and, after ten-odd years here in Manhattan, I can only say that—well—it's true: New Yorkers *are* pushier. Still, I have found them, despite some impatience and brashness, as likable and kind as people everywhere. It's hard to be in the rush of the city without being rushed yourself. When you are surrounded by lots of noise, it's hard not to raise your voice.

As soon as the race begins, White gives the following virtuoso description of the setting:

> *the seagulls wheeled and cried overhead and the taxicabs tooted and honked from Seventy-second Street and the west wind (which had come halfway across America to get to Central Park) sang and whistled in the rigging and blew spray across the decks, stinging Stuart's cheek with tiny fragments of flying peanut shell tossed up from the foamy deep.*

The Model Boat Pond is not particularly deep, but that's the point (and the joke). White is describing it from the perspective of tiny Stuart, to whom it seems as unfathomable as the Atlantic. "Rigging" is just one of many nautical words White deploys to show both how meticulously the owner has recreated a normal-sized schooner and how thoroughly Stuart knows the craft of sailing. The chapter is a humorous mishmash of sea-salty terminology and urban debris like the peanut shells. When a brown paper bag floating on the surface of the pond causes the boats to run afoul of each other, Stuart loyally obeys his captain on the shore, cuts the Wasp loose and sails to victory.

Just north of the Boat Pond there is a statue of Alice from *Alice in Wonderland* (1865). She is sitting atop a mushroom with her cat Dinah, and other famous characters, such as the Mad Hatter, the Cheshire Cat and the White Rabbit, are gathered around her. The book that introduced her to the world is generally regarded as the first children's book in our contemporary understanding of the genre. Just west of the Boat Pond, a bronze Hans Christian Andersen (1805–1875) sits reading his story, "The Ugly Duckling," to a duckling. Children can't help but climb into his lap or atop Alice's mushroom. Storytime comes alive for them here. The Model Boat Pond and its environs not only memorialize but also have generated some of the greatest literature written for the young. From the precocious boy-mouse Stuart Little we will now leap to his contemporary in fiction: the pubescent and at times purposefully immature Holden Caulfield.

With *The Catcher in the Rye* (1951), J. D. Salinger wrote not only one of the greatest novels of all time but what would become one of the most storied. Since the 1960s, it has been banned in many school districts, mostly for "foul language" but also for sexual content (including hints at homosexuality). John Hinckley Jr. claimed in 1981 that it, along with Jodie Foster, inspired him to shoot President Reagan. The book, it seems, holds a strange power to offend and possess.

J. D. Salinger grew up on Park Avenue, just east of Fifth Avenue, which runs along Central Park. He also set a short story there, "The Laughing Man" (published in 1953). He no doubt knew it well. Holden Caufield, the 16-year-old "hero" of *The Catcher in the Rye*, visits the park frequently during the four days in New York before his breakdown. On seven separate occasions in the course of the relatively short novel, Holden goes to the park mentally or physically. The park in general and the Pond along Central Park South in particular occupy vast psychic space in Holden's mind. His concern for what happens to the ducks on the Pond in the winter is an *idée fixe* for him.

He goes to the Pond mentally while "shooting the bull" with a teacher at the school from which he has been expelled:

> *The funny thing is, though, I was sort of thinking of something else while I shot the bull. I live in New York, and I was thinking of the lagoon in Central Park, down near Central Park south. I was wondering whether it would be frozen over when I got home and if it was, where did the ducks go. I was wondering where the ducks went when the lagoon got all icy and frozen over. I wondered if some guy came in a truck and took them away to a zoo or something. Or if they just flew away.*

When back in New York City, he asks two separate cabbies driving him through the park if they know what happens to the ducks:

> *You know those ducks in that lagoon right near Central Park South? That little lake? By any chance, do you happen to know where they go, the ducks, when it gets all frozen over? Do you happen to know, by any chance?*

The second cabbie, Horwitz, becomes flustered when asked about the ducks and makes an off-subject (but insistent) claim about the fish there. In a manic excitement that makes Holden fear "he was going to drive the cab into a lamppost or something," Horwitz insists the fish become fixed immovably in the ice and eat by absorbing "seaweed and crap that's in the ice" through their pores. That this is absolutely false hardly matters. Horwitz's argument, "They can't just ignore the ice," resonates on a figurative level since Holden is, like the fish described here, "frozen right in one position." He is frozen in that he cannot accept the death of his little brother Allie from leukemia three years before the events of the novel; he is frozen in that he repeats behavior (he has been expelled four times). Furthermore, that Horwitz answers a question about the ducks at the Pond by talking about the fish there fits in with Holden's theory that digressive discourse can be more interesting, aesthetically speaking, than laser-focused discourse.

Holden explains to a former teacher that Richard Kinsella, a former classmate, flunked an Oral Expression class because he would, for example, start to give a speech about his family farm and then digress, excitedly, to a story about his uncle with polio. Holden, who flunked the class as well, concludes:

> *[Kinsella's story] didn't have much to do with the farm—I admit it—but it was nice. It's nice when somebody tells you about their uncle. Especially when they start out telling you about their father's farm and then all of a sudden get more interested in their uncle.*

To expand on Holden's "nice:" an enthusiastic and spontaneous digression is more affecting than a perfunctory and prepared speech, especially when it breaks away from such a speech. In just the same way, Holden and Horwitz start out considering the ducks at the Pond, but Horwitz, excitedly, digresses to the fish. His theory of what happens to the fish in winter (they are frozen in ice) is more significant to the novel than scientific fact (they swim around under the ice). After asking Horwitz to share a drink with him (and being turned down), Holden concludes that he "was a pretty good guy. Quite amusing and all."

Holden, inebriated, finally does go to the Pond late at night to find out the answer to his question. He finds the surface half-frozen and, though he walks the whole way around the shore, sees not a single duck. The query "where do the ducks at the Pond go in the winter?" is never answered in the novel. It is so cold outside that Holden starts to become literally encased in ice: "Boy, I was still shivering like a bastard, and the back of my hair, even though I still had my hunting hat on, was sort of full of little hunks of ice." Eventually, though he only has three dollar-bills, five quarters and a nickel left, he "skips" the change across the unfrozen surface of the Pond in an intentional act of waste. He knows he will have to face his parents when the money runs out and, at this point, is hastening, rather than delaying, the inevitable.

The park operates in other ways in the novel as well. Holden's memories of his deceased brother Allie and his now ten-year-old sister Phoebe are bound up with it. In a passage describing Phoebe, we learn that the three of them regularly went to the Model Boat Pond together: "When she was a very tiny little kid, I and Allie used to take her to the park with us, especially on Sundays. Allie had this sailboat he used to like to fool around with Sundays, and we used to take Phoebe with us." They would go to the park on a Sunday, just as McGonagall and Nick Carraway did. Holden's days alone in New York

City are haunted in at least two different ways. First, wherever he goes, he is haunted by memories of Allie, of Phoebe and of others, that is, by revenants of himself and others in happier days. Second, he himself, like a ghost, revisits and haunts places where he had pleasant childhood experiences.

On a Sunday, in the hopes of seeing his sister roller-skating near the bandshell on the Mall, Holden walks into the park. His depression is becoming more and more acute, and he has started seeing ugliness everywhere around him, as he later sees "F*** you" scrawled everywhere. Salinger gives us Central Park through Holden's eyes:

> *There didn't look like there was anything in the park except dog crap and gobs of spit and cigar butts from old men, and the benches all looked like they'd be wet if you sat down on them. It made you depressed, and every once in a while, for no reason, you got goose flesh while you walked. It didn't seem at all like Christmas was coming soon. It didn't seem like anything was coming soon.*

He goes to "the same place [he] used to like to skate when [he] was a kid." There he encounters not his sister but a surrogate for and acquaintance of Phoebe. In his loneliness, he talks to her and helps her tighten her roller-skates. When he asks the ten-year-old "if she'd care to have a hot chocolate or something with [him]," he is not being creepy but curious. This novel is a rite of passage, and Holden insists on revisiting and understanding childhood thoroughly before consenting to bear the burden of maturity.

The climactic and final scene in the novel also takes place in Central Park. After deciding to hitchhike out

West, get a job and start over, Holden informs Phoebe of his intention with a note and asks to see her one final time. When she comes to meet him with luggage and insists that he take her along with him, he realizes his plan is untenable. They quarrel, and Holden uses attractions in the park—the Zoo and the Carousel—to smooth things over with her. With Phoebe still walking some distance from him, they go to the Zoo, and he stops when she stops to watch "the sea lions getting fed—a guy was throwing fish at them." Scheduled feedings of the sea lions are still a daily ritual. Holden and Phoebe are reconciled at the Carousel. Rather than joining her on it, however, he sits like a parent and watches her ride, indicating his acceptance of an adult role:

> *Then the carousel started, and I watched her go round and round...All the kids tried to grab for the gold ring, and so was old Phoebe, and I was sort of afraid she'd fall off the goddam horse, but I didn't say or do anything. The thing with kids is, if they want to grab for the gold ring, you have to let them do it, and not say anything. If they fall off, they fall off, but it is bad to say anything to them.*

The carousel that Salinger describes in this passage was destroyed by a fire in 1950, and the current one does not have a "gold" brass ring for children to reach for. But, goodness, that passage is luminous. Over the past seventy years, probably tens of thousands of high school students have written essays in which they interpret "the gold ring" as a symbol of hope. Bless them for it.

Robert Lowell's poem "Central Park" (1965) is too long to quote completely. We will focus on passages that are richest in relevance. Though "lovers" are what the eyes of the poem first focus on, the lead-up to them is anything but romantic:

Scaling small rocks, exhaling smog,
gasping at game-scents like a dog,
now light as pollen, now as white
and winded as a grounded kite—
I watched the lovers occupy
every inch of earth and sky:

Born and raised in Boston, Lowell does not have childhood memories of Central Park. To him as an adult, it is simply gritty and smelly. There is smog, which plagued New York City throughout the '60s. In one legendary toxic event in 1966, smog covered the city for three straight days over Thanksgiving weekend. Not long thereafter, President Johnson and Congress passed The Air Quality Act (1967), followed by the Clean Air Act (1970). The speaker also introduces a kite ("grounded" here), and a kite will later guide his gaze to the Obelisk. After a bleak section in which "the stain of fear and poverty" spreads over visitors to the park, Lowell takes us to the Zoo:

Drugged and humbled by the smell
of zoo-straw mixed with animal,
the lion prowled his slummy cell,
serving his life-term in jail—
glaring, grinding, on his heel,
with tingling step and testicle...

In marked contrast to McGonagall's enthusiastic take on the Menagerie, Lowell gives us a "drugged and humbled" lion as a convict with no hope of parole. Bipolar and on early psychiatric medications, Lowell may well be seeing the lion as an image of himself, with his own mental condition as a cage that feels run-down, like much of New York City was in the 1960s.

From there Lowell uses a balloon and kite, images of play, to lead the reader to the Obelisk ("Cleopatra's Needle") and through dusk to nighttime:

Shadows had stained the afternoon;
high in an elm, a snagged balloon
wooed the attraction of the moon.
Scurrying from the mouth of night,
a single, fluttery, paper kite
grazed Cleopatra's Needle, and sailed
where the light of the sun had failed.
Then night, the night—Oh jungle hour,
the rich in his slit-windowed tower…
Oh Pharaohs starving in your foxholes,
with painted banquets on the walls,
fists knotted in your captives' hair,
tyrants with little food to spare—
all your embalming left you mortal,
glazed, black, and hideously eternal,
all your plunder and gold leaf
only served to draw the thief…

At sunset the park becomes a "jungle," a metaphor that is particularly resonant during the years of the Vietnam War. Then we travel to the desert, but with lingering images of the war: the pharaohs are not buried in tombs or pyramids but "starving" in "foxholes"—a word as closely associated with the Vietnam War as trenches are with World War I. The Egyptian dolmen honoring the Pharaoh Ramses II evokes in the speaker mummified pharaohs who, through embalming, have ended up both "mortal" and "hideously eternal." Through the process of desiccation, they have not gone the way of all flesh but, after millennia, are still grotesquely present. Rather than making them wealthy in the afterlife, their burial treasures only serve "to draw the thief." The mention of graverobbers then redirects the speaker's thoughts to the muggers who might be stalking him.

In the 1960s and '70s crime was rife in New York City, and Central Park was particularly dangerous (at least 800 felonies per year). The concluding quatrain pithily portrays a '60s mindset:

We beg delinquents for our life.
Behind each bush, perhaps a knife;
each landscaped crag, each flowering shrub,
hides a policeman with a club.

Which is more to be feared, the mugger or the cop? In his poem "The March," published two years later in 1967, Lowell portrays his charge toward the Washington Monument with fellow Vietnam War protestors as a battle, with the authorities as "the other army, the Martian, the ape, the hero, / his new-fangled rifle, his green, new, steel helmet." Whereas Central Park for Lowell is consistently dangerous, dirty and decayed, it operates as a mood-ring in our next work, reflecting the main character's movement from fear and subjection to confidence and independence.

Sue Kaufman's novel, *Diary of a Mad Housewife*, (1967) is an early feminist classic. The "bored housewife" is a stock character in American literature of the '50s and

’60s, and the protagonist Tina Balser, an Upper-West-Side housewife, at first, fits that mold. Suspecting she is losing her mind, she starts a secret diary as an emotional outlet and for therapeutic purposes. Central Park is prominent in the entries, and her feelings about it gauge the development of her character. The park goes from being an acute phobia to a place where she escapes from her oppressive home life, does at long last what she wants to do and realizes who she wants to be.

Early in the novel she writes:

I’m afraid to go into the park. Today, I swore I’d make myself go in there, and got as far as the entrance when I saw the man in the middle of the path, standing up and loonily smiling up at the trees. He was a very old man with white hair, who was probably just somebody’s poor old retired Dad, or a senile bird-watcher hoping, perchance, to spot a purple finch—but I wasn’t going to risk it. Not these days. Not me.

Initially, even a harmless old man is enough to keep her from venturing in. Later she pushes herself to be brave and walks her dog in it. There she encounters “the most disgusting rat” she had ever seen. She and the rat exchange “a look of hatred so pure and intense you could almost hear it.” She admits that “part of her new looniness is the need to see signs and symbols in everything,” and that is why the rat seems “to stand for more than itself.” After she fantasizes about killing the rat and filling “the turdy grass with blood and mangled guts,” the rat disappears down a hole. She explains: “something inside me suddenly turned off, like a motor, and I felt better. It was as though that little imaginary murder had purged me.” By acknowledging that there is something unsightly and uncivilized inside of herself, she feels a kinship with the "turdy" and dangerous park and fearlessly goes deeper into it than she had gone before.

Her senses are awakening as well. On the same walk she notices how the heavy and polluted air turns the light "a thick Impressionist peachy gold" and remarks that "it was the first time in weeks [she'd] noticed anything, anything that wasn't sinister." Both the diary and the park are therapeutic for her in that they encourage her to have thoughts outside her role as housewife. She recognizes an ugliness inside of herself and the beauty of the outside world. Pleasant or unpleasant, her new thoughts are her own.

On that same walk, she is almost assaulted by a teenager. Frozen in shock before him, she is eventually saved by a neighbor walking his dogs. Later in her transformation, while she is walking through the Metropolitan Museum, a man exposes himself to her. Rather than "gasping or screaming," she bursts out laughing and mocks him as she walks away. This reaction shows the growth of her confidence. Why be squeamish? Why live in fear? Undaunted by the near assault, she cancels a dentist appointment to spend the whole day in the park: "It was a day to walk in the park, to sit in the open-air cafeteria by the boat basin, sipping a lemonade and watching the rowers on the water." She withdraws from familial obligations in order to enjoy life on her own terms.

After a snowfall in winter, she rises early and brings nuts and bits of bread for the squirrels and pigeons in the park. She describes the winter scene there as

> *what [she'd] come for: all was still, still, until a pigeon or the growing warmth of the sun would send a tatter of snow drifting down. I just stood there, smiling, until I saw about ten pigeons squatting in a tree, peering hopefully down at me, and I got to work.*

Reflecting on this experience, she writes: "I told myself that I was out there doing something I'd really wanted to do, for a change." As if she herself is using the park (and that early encounter with the rat) to gauge her transformation, she adds: "I felt so marvelous that all my stupid dreary problems had vanished—like that rat had vanished down the hole that long-ago autumn day." When she returns home, she learns that her children and husband Jonathan had been watching her in surprise and amusement through a window that faces the park. As a result of her expedition, Jonathan, not she, has made breakfast for the family. She later asserts her independence by having an affair with a playwright.

Her climactic realization also takes place in the park, on a warm day in February. Proud of overcoming her phobia, she proclaims: "Without a thought for muggers, rapists, Uncle Pee-Pees and gangs of toughs, I turned into the park and walked and walked and walked." When a "terrible exhaustion" comes over her there, she sits down and realizes: "It's over... It's really over. You're free to pick up the pieces and start again." She concludes that, whatever the future holds, "I know at least who I'm going to settle for and who I'm going to be."

The novel confronts a number of issues addressed by the goals of '60s feminism, including an end to sexual harassment and a more equitable distribution of housework and child-rearing duties. But what is most striking in this novel is Central Park operating as a metaphor for Tina's mind. As she convalesces from her malaise, it grows more and more prominent in her affection. She comes to admire the park, and she comes to respect herself. Here for the first time, we see Central Park as an escape (in this case from a humdrum existence) and an arena for personal growth.

In contrast to Teasdale's barren wintertime representation of the park, Lee Harwood (1939–2015), a prominent figure in the British Poetry Revival movement, gives us a winter scene full of "joy" and "wonder" in "Central Park Zoo" (published 1969). He is in "the great white park" (a playful alteration of "great white shark"), "looking at the zoo:" "All the animals have their thick winter coats on/– the childish humour of this is so enjoyable . . ." Harwood has, in fact, already embodied this "childhood humour" in the poem through the shark/park wordplay. His subsequent lines ("the fact we can become children again / shows how right we were in / believing in our love . . .") sum up what is, as I see it, a major purpose of the park: regression in service of the ego. According to this Freudian concept, adults "regress" to a state of childlike play, considered by some to be important in artistic creation. It is an irresponsible state, and comparatively free of inhibitions. With its many playgrounds and attractions for children, the park seems to encourage this regression in the adults who accompany them. As we have seen, part of the playfulness in question involves instant travel, through the imagination, to a distant locale.

The voice in Harwood's poem later focuses on a herd of buffalo: "there it was—the herd of buffalo / grazing on the lush plains." The Zoo had featured buffalo since the late 1800s. The most famous of them was Black Diamond (1893–1915), who was donated by the Barnum and Bailey Circus and served as the model for the image on the Buffalo Nickel. The herd evokes the "outback" of America in the speaker's mind. He goes on to describe the "teleportation" one often experiences in Central Park:

Geography in our sense is exciting
Plotting the whole course now
Sunlight and the shadows of fast

moving clouds sliding across the grassland
I imagine North Texas or even Dakota Montana

Vague to the speaker, "flyover" states like the Dakotas and Montana here fuse—and he is humorously honest about it—into a single imprecise locale: "Dakota Montana." In this vague and somewhat mythological space, the speaker finds not only a "canyon" and "plateau," but the ghosts of Native Americans: "the spirits of the tribe / waiting with a deep love for us." As we will see, the patchwork Central Park is like a sampler, not of chocolates, but of landscapes and ambiences.

In *The Prince of Central Park* (1975), Evan H. Rhodes gives us a gritty, contemporary fairy tale. Instead of a wicked stepmother, there is a physically and emotionally abusive foster mother. Our eleven-year-old hero, the orphan Jay-jay, runs away from her, dashing "out into the dawning streets to find his life." His adventures in Central Park are similar to the adventures of the scorned (and sometimes abused) youngest son in fairy tales, who seeks his fortune in a forest. After being transformed in some way, this hero emerges and rejoins society, usually in a much better living situation. Jay-jay shares the stock fairytale hero's chirpy optimism: "Maybe this is what living's all about?. . . Even when you've been knocked for a loop, if you keep your ears and eyes open, sooner or later the way to solve your problem shows up."

For all the parallels with fairy tale, however, he does not, as commonly happens in that genre, emerge from the forest and live happily ever after. Though Mrs. Miller invites the semi-feral Jay-jay to live with her, he decides to stay in the park for at least a little while longer: "I don't think I'm finished yet with what I've got to do here." It is as if Jay-jay knows that the transformation the park is meant to bring about in him is not yet completed.

The novel focuses on the north end of the park: the North Woods, the Great Hill and the Loch. Though, early on, unexplored areas of the park can turn, for Jay-jay, into the "jungle" we will encounter again in *The Park is Mine*, he almost always sees it as a solace and refuge. For example, he escapes a pursuer by running into the "the cool safety of silver birch and weeping forsythia and winding pathways." More than a refuge, though, the park is almost animate in that it provides "special protection" to Jay-jay. He concludes: "Only this park has been good to me . . . I'm going to live right here in this park! . . . Forever!" This declaration is similar to Peter Pan's insistence that he never grow up. Jay-jay will stay outside of the world, with its rules, druggies and abusers, eternally if he can.

As we have seen elsewhere, imagination and memory play over the park, whisking characters away to other places and times. Jay-jay at one point calls it "Sherwood Forest," with policemen as "the Sheriff of Nottingham's men." He thus becomes Robin Hood, a lovable rogue who steals food and other things to survive, but he has scruples: he never steals money. Sherwood Forest, like the Forest of Arden in Shakespeare's *As You Like It*, is the place where virtuous characters go to escape the wicked world and where bad guys repent or get their just desserts. The same is true here: Jay-jay leaves his abusive foster mother for the park, and his antagonist Elmo falls to his death there. Like Holden Caulfield, the elderly Mrs. Miller has fond memories of the park. These memories transform her, figuratively, into a younger version of herself: "Along the path, down the winding steps, down through the years Mrs. Miller went. Imperceptibly, her body seemed to straighten, her mid-section slimmed to an hour-glass figure." Jay-jay also "teleports" out of the park. The trees on the Great Hill become "a rainforest," another child's kite becomes enemy aircraft in a foreign war, and "the remains of a cupcake and half an orange" whisk him to England for high tea.

Crime was a concern in New York City in general and in the park in particular during the 1970s as well. Though this is a middle grade book, Jay-jay is anything but naïve. He is aware, for example, of the drug-dealing and prostitution in his foster mother's apartment complex. At 106th and Central Park West, he observes: "Rape, robbery and murder had turned this area into a no-man's-land. Even the gangs thought better of venturing here after dark." Elmo, a teenage heroin addict, serves as the villain. He hunts Jay-jay and attempts to mug Mrs. Miller. Though Jay-jay is himself quite an accomplished thief by the end of the novel, he steals for survival, not drug money. What's more, he risks exposure and his own safety to rescue Mrs. Miller when Elmo assaults her. Another hallmark of fairy tale is the hero's kindness and self-sacrifice, and Jay-jay exhibits those virtues in spades. Though the park reveals its dark side in this novel, it remains, in Jay-jay's eyes, the magical, benevolent and transformative forest of fairy tale. In the next novel we will discuss, the main character purposefully makes it malevolent, turning into a nightmare.

Like John Rambo in the film *First Blood* (1982), Harris in Stephen Peters' novel *The Park is Mine* (1981) is a haunted Vietnam vet. The book begs to be turned into a film and was, in fact, in 1985. Both novel and film make heroes of the former soldiers who drive the action, but heroism is harder to justify in the novel. Harris is an adrenaline-junkie with PTSD. While he fights for the park to recapture the rush of battle, Mitch, the vet in the film, selflessly does the same to call attention to the memory of all Vietnam vets, both the casualties and the survivors.

We have seen the park's ability to teleport visitors to faraway places, but thus far those places have not been hostile. In this novel all of Central Park is teleported to the jungles of Vietnam in wartime for six straight days:

> *Once, while standing sixty stories up on the roof of the Burlington House, with the Park stretched out below him like a big green map, Harris had been struck by the notion that Central Park was a small, incongruous country . . . Harris liked the image, because it reminded him of another small country, where everything, including himself, had been incongruous.*

Suffering a PTSD-induced hallucination near the Lake, Harris "saw a treeline on a hill; he saw a paddy wall, a dike, a black and impenetrable jungle." One general even proposes deploying "defoliate" and strafing the park with napalm to flush Harris out. To make the re-creation complete, three Vietnamese experts in guerilla warfare are eventually hired as contractors by the city to hunt Harris. Central Park thus becomes a gateway to "a parallel world."

Harris' PTSD is contagious, causing hallucinations even in people who did not fight in the war. Weaver, his hostage at first and then his lover, is an ambulance-chasing independent shooter of news footage and fellow adrenaline-junkie. Though she has never served in the military, she is herself transported through space and time to the Vietnam War: "A nightmare specter materialized in front of her. An alien, distant, forgotten war ignited and flared in the blackness. It repelled and attracted her." The police's tactical expert, Eubank, sees only hostility in the park. He is "seized by a nightmare vision of a swarming, alien enemy, something from a war he'd never experienced." When he does regress in a daydream, like Holden Caulfield, to happier days in the park, the ominous sound of incoming artillery snaps him back into the nightmare: "A memory of himself in uniform, watching kids' sail boats in the small boat pond, lingered briefly in his thoughts, only to be instantly replaced by the brutal sound of a whooshing projectile." The park, as jungle, has dark psychological powers. It not only unleashes repressed memories but imposes "alien" nightmares on people. It can teleport visitors to wars they didn't fight in and places they've never seen.

For all of this hallucination and fantasy, the novel does give us an accurate portrayal of crime in the park in the 1980s. Drug-dealing was ubiquitous; homelessness was rampant. In 1982, there were 700 robberies and nine murders. When Harris enters the park at 72nd Street and Central Park West on a Sunday evening, he describes what he sees as normal behavior there: "People congregated near the entrance at night, to sit on the benches and drink wine or to make pickups of drugs and lovers." He had also been attacked on the subway by muggers who did not survive his resistance. Throughout the novel, we encounter attractions as they were in '80s. For example, Belvedere Castle was a dilapidated storage-space for weather equipment at the time: "Graffiti covered the old stone" and "a pair of panties hung from an anemometer."

During the initial battle, the park seems so perilous to policemen who are staring "into the darkness on the other side of the wall" that "they looked as if they were waiting for a command to fire into the landscape—as if they could somehow shoot down that dangerous and implacable suspect, Central Park." Olmsted and Vaux's welcoming world of tranquility becomes an 843-acre criminal. After Harris takes the park, Dix, the liaison between the mayor and the police chief, points out an irony: "People were always complaining about how dangerous

Central Park had become. After tonight, nobody would be able to take a walk, even in the daytime." In this novel, the "dark side" of the park takes over for six days and nights. After spending time in the Vietnam War, we need a vacation. Conveniently, our next author will use the Lake in the park to take us to "the bonnie, bonnie banks of Loch Lomond."

Jay Wright (1935–) is one of the most prominent African American poets writing in America today. His work often presents loneliness and isolation, which a speaker tries to overcome through connections to an American present or an African past. We see this process at work in "The Lake in Central Park" (1988), in which a water-feature explodes with mythological significance and becomes a romance between the Lake as woman and the speaker:

It should have a woman's name,
something to tell us how the green skirt of land
has bound its hips.
When the day lowers its vermilion tapestry over the west ridge,
the water has the sound of leaves shaken in a sack,
and the child's voice that you have heard below
sings of the sea.

By slow movements of the earth's crust,
or is it that her hip bones have been shaped
by a fault of engineering?
Some coquetry cycles this blue edge,
a spring ready to come forth to correct
love's mathematics.

The Lake becomes personified as a woman in the first two stanzas. What is expressly an "it" in the opening two lines has become a "she" by line 9. As Stuart Little regards the Model Boat Pond as an ocean, so "the child's voice that you have heard below / sings of the sea" when one contemplates the Lake. Focusing on the lapping of water on the shore, the speaker wonders what causes it. Something geological like "slow movements of the earth's crust"? Something intrinsic like "her hip bones" moving? The latter, personified view wins out, it seems, because the speaker immediately sees the ripples as "coquetry."

Saturday rises immaculately.
The water's jade edge plays against corn-colored
picnic baskets, rose and lemon bottles, red balloons,
dancers in purple tights, a roan mare out of its field.
It is not the moment to think of Bahia
and the gray mother with her water explanation.
Not far from here, the city, a mass of swift water
in its own depression, licks its sores.

Everything turns colorful and playful: "the water's jade edge plays against" a list of things, each highlighted with a color word. Because of this brightness, the speaker feels the urge to teleport to "Bahia," a city in Brazil, but suppresses it: "It is not the moment to think of Bahia." There is another city, New York, "not far from here." In contrast to the fully personified Lake, New York hangs in limbo: it is something that can "lick its sores," so it has a body. Still, the city remains an "it." Furthermore, whereas the Lake flirtatiously "rises," the city is "a mass of swift water / in its own depression . . ." Other writers describe the buildings around the park as rising or even looming; here they fall away, and the Lake climbs.

Still, I would be eased by reasons.

Sand dunes in drifts.

Lava cuts its own bed at a mountain base.

Blindness enters where the light refuses to go.

In Loch Lomond, the water flowers with algae

and a small life has taken the name of a star.

Wright taught for a time in Scotland and no doubt saw Loch Lomond there firsthand. The thought of it teleports the reader from Central Park to Scotland and the largest body of freshwater in Britain. As the poet John Hollander put it, "The earth beneath Wright's poems keeps moving about." "Loch Lomond" is also the title of a well-known Scottish folk song, and its refrain hints at the travel that the speaker experiences: "O you'll take the high road and I'll take the low road, and I'll be in Scotland afore ye."

You will hear my star-slow heart

empty itself with a light-swift pitch

where the water thins to a silence.

And the woman who will not be named

screams in the birth of her fading away.

Wright uses the two words "the water" six times in a 32-line poem. By the time of its final iteration here, "the water" has moved out of any specific locale and become an elemental power. The poem ends with the water woman (the water personified), a goddess figure who is "not to be named," evanescing.

Michael Jahn has written a series of mystery novels that take legendary places in New York as their settings. Their protagonist, detective Donovan, is a native New

Yorker. Like many long-time New Yorkers he can be nostalgic, reminiscing about "the good old days" before this mayor or that mayor ruined everything. This is the first of the works we have encountered that expresses nostalgia for the Central Park of yore, though Holden Caulfield, admittedly, feels nostalgic for childhood experiences there.

In *Murder in Central Park* (2000) Donovan brings up the park's high-crime rates in the 1960s and '70s: "you know Central Park is a lot safer than it was during the days Johnny Carson used to make fun of it." He expresses half-ironic nostalgia for a pre-gentrification New York City. For example, when given an address in the Morningside neighborhood, he says, "The last neighborhood in Manhattan to escape gentrification . . . It's still possible to get coffee and a doughnut for a buck from the bodega or buy grass from a kid who brings it to your car. Or look out the living room window and watch an old-fashioned gunfight between drug-lords." The park itself also regresses thirty or forty years. Donovan sees a "retro crowd" in it, whose "boom box blasted disco hits from the 1970s." Roller-skating, so important in *The Catcher in the Rye* and especially popular in the '70s, is frequent in the novel.

Though the park is only 166 years old and, for the most part, artificially landscaped, Jahn sees the "antediluvian" in it. At times the park becomes Nature itself. We meet several characters who, like Jay-jay in *The Prince of Central Park*, live in it, and one of them, the poet and sage known as "Milton," aspires to "live within nature" and is answering the "call of the wild." There is a running joke about wolves living in the park. Donovan laughingly dismisses rumors of them as urban legend until he encounters one there himself. The wolves become a symbol of the wildness of the park: "The howling that you hear every full moon isn't junkies wailing from behind the cold stone walls of Belvedere Castle, it's a wolf pack on the prowl by the banks of the Harlem Meer."

The park teleports Donovan to various New World settings, both North and South American: "Iowa," "The Continental Divide," and "a wild and rocky zone. . . resembling scenery found off the beaten path in Vermont." Despite the many resident characters he encounters there, the park can even be a desert and "bed of solitude." At times, the take on the park in this novel is similar to Old World myths about the New World. It is a "forest primeval" where one can hear "primal cries of alarm" from crows and encounter people sitting Indian-style who "huddle like the Mohave." We even learn about the Ishimani, a fictional Amazonian tribe, and rituals they perform involving, first, the ingestion of a poisonous tree frog's venom, then human sacrifice. The murder weapon, a distinctive ritual knife, was designed for just that purpose. One of Donovan's colleagues even makes the comparison between the park and Amazonian rain forest explicit: "I used to work in the Amazon Jungle . . . I think I can handle Central Park." Donovan's retort ("think again") implies that the urban jungle is even more dangerous than a real one. In the end, though, all the hints at savagery and ceremonies of blood and venom turn out to be red herrings—the inept culprit killed the victim by mistake, thinking he was the man that cuckolded him. Our next author also sees the "primitive" in the park.

Katherine Barrett Swett's poem "Central Park Zoo, 1970" (published in 2015) develops the theme of nostalgia for the park, felt by Holden Caulfield when he yearns for the happier days of his childhood, and Donovan when he misses the crime-ridden yet somehow more authentic 1970s in New York. As we have seen, one need not feel nostalgia only for pleasant times and experiences.

One can miss not just the quaint dinginess of a certain place but even the excitement of the hazards there. So, in this poem, the speaker travels backward through forty-five years to a time when the Central Park Zoo was run-down.

Back in the old zoo—the place the child
of New York's Parks commissioner once called
Sing-Sing for beasts, where elephants and wild
cats, bears and rhinos were all jailed,
sliced into strips of pacing fur, the shriek
and stink of monkeys everywhere, a mess—
it was not pastoral or picturesque,
and unprotected by a wilderness,
forced to face a hungry, hot stare,
we felt them close and thought, we are like this,
monkeys fighting, lions with twitching haunches,
their paunches swinging; and while we ate our lunches,
children circled round the chipped green benches,
taunting each other, "you belong in there."

As the animals become human by being "jailed" instead of "caged," so the children become animals. "Sing-Sing" refers to the Correctional Facility that hosted New York's execution chamber until capital punishment ended in the state in 2004. "Old Sparky," the electric chair there, was the last seat for many high-profile criminals, including Julius and Ethel Rosenberg, convicted of selling nuclear secrets to the Soviet Union. There is great irony in referring to a place that housed inmates condemned to death as a "Correctional Facility" or even a

"Penitentiary." With no chance of escaping their cages and running free in the wild, the animals themselves are figuratively on death row.

The sonnet effectively captures the "mess" that the Zoo was in the late 1960s and '70s. As inmates of Sing-Sing in those years suffered through notoriously harsh conditions (made worse by an economic crisis), so the animals in the Zoo here must endure cramped cages and the reek of manure. By 1967, for example, the wooden railings on the fences were rotting. In 1976 a report from the World Federation for the Protection of Animals concluded that the Central Park Zoo was operating in "shameful conditions." At the same time subway lines for the F and Q trains were being built beneath it, and the "graffiti wall" in a tunnel served as a gathering place for early subway artists such as Ali, who dubbed the site "Zoo York." Given the themes of this poem, Zoo York is a particularly apt nickname because the children live in the city and feel that their classmates "belong" in small and squalid cages like the beasts they are viewing. Furthermore, given the small size of most New York apartments and the often sordid buildings into which they are packed, many New Yorkers themselves may as well be living in stacked cages. The Zoo described in this poem was closed for renovations in 1983 and the current iteration opened in 1988.

In his novel, *Central Park* (2021), Guillaume Musso, a popular French writer of suspense, makes use of the park's uncanny ability to evoke other places in the minds of visitors. He also, implicitly, compares the complex network that is the park to the human neural network. As the main character Alice Schafer is "out of time" and "outside of time" in a variety of senses, so the Ramble, where she regains consciousness at the beginning of the novel, is a "a place removed from time."

After going out with girlfriends for a night on the town in Paris, Alice, a French detective, wakes up spattered with blood and handcuffed to a stranger with one bullet missing from the gun in her pocket and no recollection of how she got there. On waking she finds herself in a "forest, the leaves on the trees autumn gold, the undergrowth fresh and dense." That forest is Central Park (specifically the Ramble), but she sees the French "forest of Rambouillet" in it. The stranger, a jazz musician named Gabriel who claims he had played a gig in Dublin the night before, insists it is "Wicklow," a national park in southern Ireland. Before they recognize the Bow Bridge and realize they are in Central Park, their surroundings are "a wooded labyrinth," a puzzle to solve in the same way as the pair must solve the mystery of their forgotten movements.

When Alice's Alzheimer's is revealed later in the novel, the wooded labyrinth becomes a metaphor for the maze of the human mind. Whereas Holden Caulfield goes to the park out of nostalgia for childhood experiences there, and Harris goes there to reenact traumatic memories of the Vietnam War, Alice begins her quest to reconstruct her memory in it, as if the trails were neurons, and the crossroads, synapses. When Gabriel who, as it turns out, is a psychologist specializing in memory loss, walks into the Ramble, he contrasts the fading noise of the city with the growing sound of birds and trees:

> *It was hard to believe that a dense forest could exist so close to a busy area. The thicker the vegetation grew, the quieter the sounds of the city became, and finally they disappeared altogether. Soon, all he could hear was birdsong and the rustle of leaves.*

As he disappears into the park, the honks, sirens and general loudness of a city of over six million give way to "birdsong and the rustle of leaves." Those sounds are not outside of but, here, inside of human civilization in the same way as meditation takes place inside of a physical body. In this novel, the park is both a riddle and its answer.

We have seen Central Park as a primitive space, a romantic getaway, a portal to other locales and times and, finally, as the human mind itself. Musso's metaphor is particularly resonant in that it is through the interplay of the park as object and the human mind as subject that all of the other associations can occur. Guidebooks can give us maps of the park and, say, help us identify the bird species in it, but only through imagination does it become "a savage place . . . holy and enchanted" or a pastoral paradise or the Midwest or the Far East. If Central Park were a mental process, it would be imagination itself.

INDEX

ABOUT THE AUTHOR

Aaron Poochigian earned a PhD in classics from the University of Minnesota and an MFA in poetry from Columbia University. In the award-winning poetry collections *Manhattanite* (2017) and *American Divine* (2021), he captures the sensory details of New York City, sublimating them to epiphanies and revelations. His poems have appeared in such publications as *The Best American Poetry*, *The Paris Review*, and *Poetry*.

A recipient of an NEA Grant in translation, he has published translations with Penguin Classics and W. W. Norton, including the popular *Sappho: Stung with Love* (2009) and Baudelaire's *The Flowers of Evil* (2021). His translation of Euripides' tragedy *Bacchae* received national acclaim when it was produced at the Getty Villa, BAM, and the Guthrie Theatre in 2019–2020. In his original poetry and translations, he is especially interested in bringing the incantatory power of poetry to a wider audience.

ABOUT FAMILIUS

Visit Our Website: www.familius.com

Familius is a global trade publishing company that publishes books and other content to help families be happy. We believe that happy families are key to a better society and the foundation of a happy life. We recognize that every family looks different and passionately believe in helping all families find greater joy, whatever their situation. To that end, we publish beautiful books that help families live our 10 Habits of Happy Family Life: *love together, play together, learn together, work together, talk together, heal together, read together, eat together, give together,* and *laugh together*. Further, Familius does not discriminate on the basis of race, color, religion, gender, age, nationality, disability, caste, or sexual orientation in any of its activities or operations. Founded in 2012, Familius is located in Sanger, California.

Connect

Facebook: www.facebook.com/familiusbooks

Pinterest: www.pinterest.com/familiusbooks

Instagram: @FamiliusBooks

TikTok: @FamiliusBooks

The most important work you ever do will be within the walls of your own home.